G000298916

TRAUMA AND
ATTACHMENT

The Centre for Attachment-based Psychoanalytic Psychotherapy

TRAUMA AND ATTACHMENT

THE JOHN BOWLBY MEMORIAL CONFERENCE MONOGRAPH 2006

Edited by

Sarah Benamer and Kate White

Published by
KARNAC

Published in 2008 by
Karnac Books Ltd
118 Finchley Road, London NW3 5HT

Copyright © 2008 The Centre for Attachment-based Psychoanalytic Psychotherapy

Individual contributions copyright © 2008 to the contributors

The rights of the contributors to be identified as the authors of this work have been asserted with §§77 and 78 of the Copyright Design and Patents Act 1988.

All rights reserved. No part of this publication may be reproduced, stored in a retrieval system, or transmitted, in any form or by any means, electronic, mechanical, photocopying, recording, or otherwise, without the prior written permission of the publisher.

British Library Cataloguing in Publication Data

A C.I.P. for this book is available from the British Library

ISBN 978 1 85575 666 3

Edited, designed, and produced by The Studio Publishing Services Ltd
www.publishingservicesuk.co.uk
e-mail: studio@publishingservicesuk.co.uk

Printed and bound in Great Britain by the MPG Books Group

www.karnacbooks.com

CONTENTS

Sarah Benamer is a member of the Centre for Attachment-based Psychoanalytic Psychotherapy (CAPP), where she is a tutor and teacher. She works as a relational psychotherapist in private practice and has a particular interest in trauma and the body. Prior to training as a psychotherapist she was an independent advocate working to support those in crisis within the National Health Service (NHS) Psychiatric System and for people with physical disabilities.

Bernice Laschinger had many years of experience in community mental health prior to becoming an attachment-based psychoanalytic psychotherapist. She is a member of CAPP, where she is a training therapist and supervisor, and has been very involved in the development of CAPP's innovative training curriculum, particularly with the integration of the relational model of psychoanalysis into the course.

Chris Purnell trained as a psychotherapist with CAPP. He currently works in the National Health Service (NHS) and maintains a small private practice. His particular interest is in working with trauma using an attachment perspective, and he has extensive experience in working with people who are facing life-threatening illness as well as with adult survivors of childhood sexual abuse. He has developed group psychotherapy within the NHS for refugees and asylum seekers who are suffering from the enduring traumatic effects of imprisonment, torture, and forced separation from their secure base. Chris has presented papers on his work at national and international conferences, and has published several papers in journals and books.

Sue Richardson is an attachment-based psychotherapist with over 30 years experience in the helping professions. Her personal and professional attachment networks are in the north-east of England, where she is based. Sue is a part of an international network of professionals who have pioneered awareness of child sexual abuse. She has integrated her extensive knowledge of child abuse into her work with adults who have suffered attachment trauma, and she has a special interest in the study and treatment of dissociation.

Valerie Sinason is a member of CAPP, a poet, psychoanalyst, and child psychotherapist. She is Director of the Clinic for Dissociative Studies and Honorary Consultant Psychotherapist to the Cape Town Child Guidance Clinic, University of Cape Town. Specializing in disability, trauma, and abuse, Valerie has published extensively in the field as well as having two full-length poetry collections published. She was formerly a Consultant Child Psychotherapist at the Tavistock Clinic, Anna Freud Clinic and Portman Clinic, and a Consultant Research Psychotherapist at St George's Hospital Medical School Psychiatry of Disability Department until December 2006. She is President of the Institute for Psychotherapy and Disability.

Gillian Slovo was born in South Africa and is the author of a family memoir, *Every Secret Thing*, and eleven novels. Her novel *Red Dust*, a story about the impact of the Truth and Reconciliation Commission on a backwater town in the semi desert Karoo (SA), won the French RFI Temoin du Monde prize, and has become a feature film starring Hilary Swank and Chiwetel Ejiofor. Her penultimate novel, *Ice Road*, was short listed for the Orange Prize. Gillian is also co-author of the play *Guantanamo: Honour-Bound to Defend Freedom*, which has played in, among other places, London, New York, Stockholm, and Washington. Her new novel, *If Wishes Were Horses*, will be published in 2008.

Bessel van der Kolk has been active as a clinician, researcher, and teacher in the area of post traumatic stress for thirty years. He founded the first clinic that specializes exclusively in the treatment of traumatized children and adults in 1982 in Boston. His current research is on how trauma affects memory processes, brain-imaging studies of PTSD, treatment outcome of EMDR vs. pharmacological interventions, the effects of theatre groups on preventing violence among chronically traumatized young people, and various ways in which traumatized individuals can actively control their own physiological states, such as yoga. He helped found the National Child Traumatic Stress Network in the USA, and is Professor of Psychiatry at Boston University Medical School, Past President of the International Society of Traumatic Stress, and Clinical Director of the Trauma Center in Boston.

Kate White is a training therapist, supervisor, and teacher at the Centre for Attachment-based Psychoanalytic Psychotherapy. Formerly senior lecturer at South Bank University in the Department of Nursing and Community Health Studies, she has used her extensive experience in adult education to contribute to the innovative psychotherapy curriculum developed at CAPP. In addition to working as an individual psychotherapist, Kate runs workshops on the themes of attachment and trauma in clinical practice. Informed by her experience of growing up in South Africa, she has long been interested in the impact of race and culture on theory and on clinical practice.

Rachel Wingfield is the Chair of the Centre for Attachment-based Psychoanalytic Psychotherapy, where she is also a training supervisor and teacher. Rachel has a wide range of clinical experience in a variety of settings, including forensic ones. She has specialized in working with survivors of trauma and abuse, including sexual abuse, rape, domestic violence, war, state terror, torture, and organized abuse. She has a particular interest in concepts of diagnostic labelling, "unsuitability" and "untreatability" in relation to psychotherapy and how they are used to distance us from working towards change with traumatized people. Rachel has been a psychotherapist with the Clinic for Dissociative Studies, since 2001. She trained at CAPP and is a training therapist, teacher, and supervisor. She has experience in a wide range of clinical settings, including within institutions and the voluntary sector, and currently works as a psychotherapist in private practice, as well as in prisons. Rachel has a particular interest in working clinically with issues of sexuality, violence, and abuse.

Felicity de Zulueta is a Consultant Psychiatrist in Psychotherapy and lead clinician of the Traumatic Stress Service at the Maudsley Hospital. She is also Honorary Senior Lecturer at King's College London, a group analyst, systemic therapist, and psychoanalytic psychotherapist. Author of numerous papers and lectures on attachment and PTSD, she outlined the case for PTSD as an attachment disorder in her book *From Pain to Violence, The Traumatic Origins of Destructiveness* [2nd edition by John Wiley and Sons, (2006) Chichester].

ACKNOWLEDGEMENTS

Thanks to the Bowlby Memorial Conference 2006 Planning Group: Judith Erskine, Richard Bowlby, and Judy Yellin for their creative work in producing a stimulating and ground-breaking conference which has enabled the emergence of this exciting and timely monograph. A special thank you to all the contributors to the conference whose innovative work can now reach a much wider audience.

Thanks to our 13th John Bowlby Memorial Lecturer 2006, Bessel van der Kolk, for his imaginative and moving presentation, which provided a context for the leading-edge clinical discussions emerging out of this conference.

A very special thank you to Grayson Perry for his very generous gift of the image for the cover of this book. It was chosen especially to reflect the complexity and depth of the painful themes explored in this monograph.

A special thank you to Oliver Rathbone for his continuing belief in the value of publishing these monographs and to Christelle Yeyet-Jacquot at Karnac Books for their patience and support in the production and publication process.

Sarah Benamer and Kate White
November 2007

Trauma and attachment

Introduction to the monograph of The 13th John Bowlby Memorial Conference 2006

Sarah Benamer and Kate White

The planning of the John Bowlby Memorial Conference is a pleasure to be a part of. It is an organic process through which we as conference organisers share our clinical work, theoretical understanding, our questions about what might be missing in the literature, and what may contribute to a deeper appreciation of our clients and ourselves. The 2006 conference, part of a series that includes "Unmasking race, culture, and attachment in the psychoanalytic space" and "Shattered states—disorganized attachment and its repair", evolved out of our response to clients who have sought our help in their bid to survive vivid experiences of trauma in all its various forms, whether endured first hand or transmitted intergenerationally. This monograph continues that journey of exploration.

As this suggests, we live in troubled times. Perhaps this has always been so, but this moment in history seems a particularly poignant one for therapists to reflect on how we may understand trauma and find meaning in the desolation, individually and in the wider sphere, as community members who may be able to contribute something very particular to the debate.

1

Underpinning our endeavour to promote social inclusion at The John Bowby Centre, is the understanding that trauma and the potential disruption of our attachment bonds are at the heart of human experience. This monograph explores our questions about the relational and interpersonal aspects of the links between attachment and trauma as they emerge in clinical practice, together with ways in which trauma is experienced emotionally and physically in the body and how this might be expressed interpersonally in the therapeutic encounter. This is discussed through personal and clinical narratives of leading researchers, clinicians, and writers.

We are defining trauma as the exposure to life-threatening experiences (actual or perceived) where a person is faced with overwhelming feelings of helplessness and terror at the possibility of annihilation: life and death moments, accompanied by abandonment, isolation, hopelessness, shame, and invisibility. These include experiences that engender a fear of disintegration and threaten a person's psychic survival far beyond the moment of actual threat.

The spectrum of trauma the contributors seek to elucidate ranges from cumulative relational trauma in a family setting, to sexual and physical abuse, to war and natural disasters. Through the inclusion of individual narratives of trauma, we are told stories that lead us into the process of survival and remind us of human tenacity and dignity in the face of overwhelming trauma. Contributors discuss survival strategies, attempts to soothe and regulate our terror states, ranging from dissociation to repression and substance abuse. Themes of secrecy, disavowal, and repetition are encountered as aspects of the complex ways in which we are able to adapt and evolve in response to adversity. The impact of trauma on our emotional and bodily states, as well as how it ruptures whole communities, are part of our conversation. Neuroscience and findings about how traumatic experience is processed and stored psychically and bodily contribute to our perception of what may be possible in clinical practice and how trauma-focused work may differ from more classical models in technique and approach.

Gillian Slovo weaves a personal and political narrative of living through the large-scale trauma of apartheid in South Africa, helping us to understand a culture of trauma and to think about how whole communities recover from disintegration of this nature. What empowers recovery and reparation on a personal level (emotional and bodily) as well as repair of the social fabric? Can the two be achieved through the same process?

Chris Purnell, in describing his upbringing in a children's home in Britain, explores the effect of racism, isolation, and loss of attachment on developing a sense of self and belonging, and how this in turn enriches his appreciation of those with whom he works clinically.

Bessel van der Kolk, author of *Traumatic Stress* and a renowned researcher who has pioneered work in this field, discusses the new diagnostic category of "Developmental trauma disorder". In contemplating the impact of trauma developmentally, he contributes to our knowledge of the ways in which traumatic encounters have profound structural ramifications and consequently negative influence on our capacity to be in the world at different stages of the life cycle.

What promotes recovery, transformation, and personal reconnection is, of course, a crucial question. Sue Richardson and Rachel Wingfield explore through clinical accounts the process of repair in the context of an ongoing long-term attachment relationship. They investigate how it may be possible for a client, through engagement with an attuned and responsive other, to find a home for the complexity of their life story internally and in the world; to find meaning in a new sense of belonging and being loved.

In considering the nature of the therapeutic dyad in relation to trauma, Valerie Sinason offers some perspectives on the impact of trauma on the therapist. She explores the possibilities of secondary traumatization and how we may best take care of ourselves and, by doing so, continue as a secure base for those we seek to empower.

The conference attracted people from all sectors of the community whose work involves counselling and therapy relationships with people who have been traumatized. In the spirit of an ongoing process, it is hoped that this monograph will continue to encourage us to question, and to further the understanding of, trauma; to remember, bear witness, and encourage hope.

Attachment theory and The John Bowlby Memorial Lecture 2006

A short history

Bernice Laschinger

T he theme of this year's Bowlby Conference links directly with the inspirational core of Bowlby's thinking. His early experience of children displaced through war or institutionalization led him to the conviction that the heart of traumatic experience lay in parental loss and prolonged separation from caregivers. These observations laid the foundations of attachment theory. Later, however, in trying to account for the continuity of these experiences into adulthood, Bowlby came to the understanding that the complexities of the traumatic impact on the child's development could only be fully understood in the context of its relationship with parents. The essential significance of traumatic experience lay in the "unravelling of the relationship between self and nurturing other, the very fabric of psychic life".

In the 1970s and 1980s, the increased awareness of the extent of childhood physical and sexual abuse formed the background to deepened understanding of trauma within attachment research. Abused children were not only threatened by the loss of their secure base, but were also faced with a more profound conflict when their attachment figures became sources of danger. Since then, the core insights of attachment theory have been incorporated into other

5

cognitive, social-psychiatric, and neurobiological approaches to trauma. In this integration, the work of this year's Bowlby Memorial Lecturer, Bessel van der Kolk, has been ground-breaking. While demonstrating the limitations of current formulations of post trau-matic stress in terms of single catastrophic events, his work opens windows on the devastating emotional and physiological conse-quences of cumulative relational trauma on human development.

This core understanding is implicit in Bowlby's earliest works. His post-war studies of refugee children led to the publication of his seminal work, *Maternal Care and Mental Health* by the World Health Organization in 1952. The documented and filmed sequence of chil-dren's responses to separation in terms of protest, detachment, and despair, as researched by James Robertson, provided evidence of separation anxiety. The impact of these ideas on the development of care of children in hospital has been enormous. The 2001 Bowlby Lecturer, Michael Rutter, discussed institutional care and the role of the state in promoting recovery from neglect and abuse. His lecture was a testament to the continuing relevance of Bowlby's thinking to contemporary social issues.

Although Bowlby joined the British Psychoanalytic Society in the 1930s and received his training from Joan Riviere and Melanie Klein, he became increasingly sceptical of their focus on the inner fantasy life of the child rather than real life experience, and tended towards what would now be termed a relational approach. Thus, in searching for a theory that could explain the anger and distress of separated young children, Bowlby turned to disciplines outside psychoanalysis, such as ethology. He became convinced of the rele-vance of animal, and particularly primate, behaviour to our under-standing of the normal process of attachment. These relational concepts presented a serious challenge to the closed world of psychoanalysis in the 1940s, and earned Bowlby the hostility of his erstwhile colleagues for several decades.

The maintenance of physical proximity by a young animal to a preferred adult is found in a number of animal species. This suggested to Bowlby that attachment behaviour has a survival value, the most likely function of which is that of care and protec-tion, particularly from predators. It is activated by conditions such as sickness, fear, and fatigue. Threat of loss leads to anxiety and anger; actual loss to anger and sorrow. When efforts to restore the bond fail, attachment behaviour may diminish, but will persist at an unconscious level and may become reactivated by reminders of the lost adult, or new experiences of loss.

Attachment theory's basic premise is that, from the beginning of life, the baby human has a primary need to establish an emotional bond with a care-giving adult. Attachment is seen as a source of human motivation as fundamental as those of food and sex. Bowlby (1979, p. 129) postulated that

> Attachment behaviour is any form of behaviour that results in a person attaining or maintaining proximity to some other preferred and differentiated individual . . . While especially evident during early childhood, attachment behaviour is held to characterise human beings from the cradle to the grave.

Attachment theory highlights the importance of mourning in relation to trauma and loss. An understanding of the relevance of this to therapeutic practice was a vital element in the foundation of the Centre for Attachment-based Psychoanalytic Psychotherapy (CAPP). The consequences of disturbed and unresolved mourning processes was a theme taken up by Colin Murray Parkes when he gave the first John Bowlby Memorial Lecture in 1993.

Mary Ainsworth, an American psychologist who became Bowlby's lifelong collaborator, established the interconnectedness between attachment behaviour, care-giving in the adult, and exploration in the child. While the child's need to explore and the need for proximity might seem contradictory, they are, in fact, complementary. It is the mother's provision of a secure base, to which the child can return after exploration, which enables the development of self-reliance and autonomy. Ainsworth developed the Strange Situation Test for studying individual differences in the attachment patterns of young children. She was able to correlate these to their mothers' availability and responsiveness. Her work provided both attachment theory and psychoanalysis with empirical support for some basic premises. This provided the necessary link between attachment concepts and their application to individual experience in a clinical setting.

Over the past two decades, the perspective of attachment theory has been greatly extended by the work of Mary Main, who was another Bowlby Memorial Lecturer. She developed the Adult Attachment Interview in order to study the unconscious processes that underlie the behavioural pattern of attachment identified by Mary Ainsworth. Further support came from the perspective of infant observation and developmental psychology developed by yet another Bowlby Lecturer, Daniel Stern. The Bowlby Lecturer for 2000, Allan Schore, presented important developments in the new field of neuro-psychoanalysis, describing emerging theories of how attachment experiences in early life shape the developing brain.

The links beween attachment theory and psychoanalysis have also been developed. Jo Klein, a great supporter of CAPP and also a former contributor to the Bowlby Conference, has explored these links in psychotherapeutic practice. In particular, the 1998 Bowlby Lecturer, Stephen Mitchell, identified a paradigm shift away from drive theory within psychoanalysis. His proposed "relational matrix" links attachment theory to other relational psychoanalytic theories that find so much resonance in the current social and cultural climate. Within this area of convergence between attachment research and developmental psychoanalysis, the 1999 Bowlby Lecturer, Peter Fonagy, has developed the concept of "mentalization", extending our understanding of the importance of the reflective function, particularly in adversity.

In similar vein, the work of Beatrice Beebe, the 2001 Bowlby Lecturer, represents another highly creative development in the unfolding relational narrative of the researcher–clinician dialogue. Her unique research has demonstrated how the parent–infant interaction creates a distinct system, organized by mutual influence and regulation, which is reproduced in the adult therapeutic relationship.

In the movement to bring the body into the forefront of relational theory and practice, the 2003 Bowlby Lecturer, Susie Orbach, has been a leading pioneer. It was the publication of her groundbreaking books, *Fat is a Feminist Issue* and *Hunger Strike* that introduced a powerful and influential approach to the study of the body in its social context. Over the past decade, one of her major interests has been the construction of sexuality and bodily experience in the therapeutic relationship.

The 2004 Bowlby Lecturer, Jody Messler Davies, has made major contributions to the development of the relational model. Her integration of trauma theory and relational psychoanalysis led to new understandings of the transference–countertranference as a vehicle for expressing traumatic experience.

Our last Bowlby Lecturer in 2005, Kimberlyn Leary, illuminated the impact of racism on the clinical process. The importance of her contribution lay in her understanding of the transformative potential inherent in the collision of two "racialized subjectivities" in the therapeutic process. She showed the possibility for reparation when both therapist and client break the silence surrounding their difference

The contribution of this year's Bowlby Lecturer to the understanding of post traumatic stress has been seminal. As researcher, clinician, and teacher, he has been one of its foremost pioneers. His 1987 book, *Psychological Trauma*, was the first to consider the impact of trauma on the entire person. He achieved this by integrating neurobiological, interpersonal, and social perspectives. This is an approach that has had enormous influence on researchers and clinicians alike. The breadth of his understanding is also reflected in his recent work, which seeks to expand the range of traditional therapies to include working with bodily states and action in the treatment of trauma.

References

Bowlby, J. (1952). *Maternal Care and Mental Health* (2nd edn), World Health Organisation: Monograph Series No. 2. Geneva: World Health Organisation.

Bowlby, J. (1979). *The Making and Breaking of Affectional Bonds*. London: Tavistock.

Davies, J. M., & Frawley, M. G. (1994). *Treating the Adult Survivor of Childhood Sexual Abuse: A Psychoanalytic Perspective*. New York: Basic Books.

Holmes, J. (1993). *John Bowlby and Attachment Theory*. London: Routledge.

Howell, E. F. (2002). Back to the "States". *Psychoanalytic Dialogues*, *12*(6): 921–957.

van der Kolk, B. (1987). *Psychological Trauma*. Washington, DC: American Psychiatric Press.

van der Kolk B. (1989). The compulsion to repeat the trauma. *Psychiatric Clinics of North America*, *12*(2): 389–411.

van der Kolk, B. (2005). Developmental trauma disorder: towards a rational diagnosis for children with complex trauma histories. *Psychiatric Annals*, *25*(5): 401–408.

Truth and reconciliation?

Gillian Slovo

B etween 1994 and 1995, I lived in Cape Town, researching what was to become my family memoir. This was the first occasion in over thirty years that I had spent any protracted time in South Africa (for almost thirty I had not been able to go back). It was a wonderful year to be there. The best. South Africa's democratic election was held in April of 1994, and, despite the fears of violence in the run-up, and even, possibly, civil war, the election had gone as smoothly and also as movingly as any election the world had witnessed.

The African National Congress (ANC) was now in power. Nelson Mandela was South Africa's first democratically elected president. His, and his party's aim, was to turn a country from the "skunk" of the world, into a model whose watchwords were equality, justice, and reconciliation.

Welcome to the new South Africa.

And here is a story from that time (although it isn't fiction).

It was in January 1995, nine months after the election, that I was pushing a trolley round a Sea Point supermarket. As I moved into the dried fruits section, I overheard four Sea Point ladies (and I use this term knowingly, so as to conjure up for you what kind of women they were). They were complaining about the recent changes to what was then South Africa's equivalent of Radio 4's *Today* programme. They didn't like the local focus (for local, read black) of the news. They didn't like the way it was biased. And, "What's worse," one of them said, to the accompaniment of the others' nods, "I can't even understand them half the time. I mean, the bulletins are read by an American woman, and a you-know-what."

I couldn't resist. I stopped my trolley, and said, in my best English accent, "Excuse me, but I couldn't help overhearing. I'm from England. You used a phrase I've not heard before. What exactly is a you-know-what?"

They shuffled around, embarrassed, one of them saying they couldn't possibly tell me. But another was bolder.

"It's a black," she said.

I told them how shocked I was that they were talking this way, given all that had happened. But they were a match for my superior English ways. "You can be shocked as you like," one of them said. "We don't care. It's a free country and we are free to say what we want."

Welcome to the new South Africa, where the old uses the new freedoms to justify itself.

Let me just quickly sum up what the old South Africa was. It was a country run by the white minority National Party, whose ruling principle was apartheid—a system of inequality enshrined in law. A system that the United Nations called a "crime against humanity". A system where every aspect of every life was determined by skin colour. Where the majority, Africans, were dispossessed of their land, and left almost entirely without rights. Where they, alone, were made to carry passes that dictated where they could live, where they could work, and where their families would have to be. It was a country where servants were cheap, and where every highly privileged "white" city or hamlet would have a township to service it. In those townships "blacks" only would live, people one on top of each other, most often without electricity, sanitation, or running water. Where the economically inactive were relegated to the Bantustans (also called, in good old-fashioned South African double speak, homelands), which were the bleakest and least fertile sections of the country, and where infant mortality rates were sky high.

I could go on, but I'm sure it's not necessary. I'm sure most of you know about apartheid South Africa. The reason I've even bothered with this sketchiest of summations is that I, and every South African, is conscious that the new South Africa is now more than ten years old. From outside, and from inside stable Britain, that might seem like no time at all. But in South Africa, where, as in so many other southern nations, the population is so young, there is now a generation of adults whose consciousness and expectations have been defined, not by apartheid (as mine were), but by the rainbow nation. And there is another up-and-coming generation, the "born free", to whom apartheid seems like ancient history, just as, in my day, because we were allowed so little real history, we thought ancient history was Jan van Riebeck rounding the Cape.

I am a novelist and my work-face is my imagination, but that imagination is fed both by experience and by what is happening out in the world. Memory, and the way it changes, and its large-scale cohort, history, and the way it can be reinterpreted, fascinate my novelist's eye. If writers can be said to mine particular themes and particular sets of problematics that surround those themes, then my theme would be how we carry our past into our present, and how, by doing this, we change our pasts.

The source of my fascination is my own past. I am one of three daughters of two parents, both of whom were prominent in South Africa's struggle against apartheid. My father, Joe Slovo, who, in the 1980s, was the Chief of Staff of the ANC's army, Umkhonto we'Sizwe (*MK*), became, in 1994, Mandela's first Housing Minister, a position Joe held until his death from cancer. My mother, Ruth First, a writer, academic, and prominent anti-apartheid activist, never lived to see the new South Africa. She was killed, in 1982, by a letter bomb that had been sent to her by the South African security police.

When I was a child, almost everything my parents did was illegal. As a result, my childhood was shot through with secrets. Since the not knowing was almost as scary as the knowledge itself, I became an expert eavesdropper. Secrets not only interested me; they held me in their thrall. No surprise, then, that when I first started writing I wrote detective novels: for what is a detective other than a person who is trying to uncover things that other people are trying to keep from her?

But fast-forward with me now to that other moment in time. Post apartheid, 1995, and I was in South Africa to research my family memoir. The underground struggle, which included the military struggle in which my father had played such a pivotal role, was over. The secrets that had dogged my childhood were no longer dangerous. Here was my chance to uncover them.

But, before I could, I found myself having to struggle with my own internal prohibitions. I had spent so much of my life knowing I shouldn't ask that I now found it difficult to break the taboo. That external need for secrecy had become my own internal censorship. Over and over again I had to struggle with myself to actually ask.

And I wasn't alone in this. Those I interviewed (and I'm talking in the main about people who had been involved in the ANC, and in the underground struggle) fell into two broad categories.

like Holocaust survivors

There were the ones who still wouldn't talk; who would never talk; who had learned the art of secrecy, and saw no reason to unlearn it. This attitude was brought to me most comically by somebody high up in Intelligence who, I heard, had instructed an underling: "Gillian Slovo is coming round to ask questions. Answer all of them, but please, don't tell her anything."

And then there were the people who got relief from finally being able to talk. Many of these had also spent the years of apartheid in the ANC underground. Their lives had also been punctuated by losses that, because of circumstances, they were not able to mourn. Remember: the struggle against apartheid was bloody and one-sided. Members of MK, had to grow accustomed to the loss of their comrade soldiers who had gone into the country, as well as to the loss of people like my mother, killed by the South African regime's assassination policy. And, inside the country, the black population was witness to disappearances, extra-judicial killings by the police, as well as full-scale armed assault on unarmed children, the like of which occurred in 1976, with the resulting loss of thousands of young lives.

If, at the time when all this was going on, people had fully taken in the extent of these losses, they might not have been able to continue. Thus was the ANC slogan, "Don't mourn. Mobilize", born. It was a product of political necessity.

But back to 1995. That phase of history was over, and there was time, if not exactly to mourn, then at least to face, more fully, some of the losses endured. And thus it was that I interviewed people to whom the simplest question would act as the opening of the flood-gates of memory, most of which was full of the horrors of what they had witnessed.

The kind of things that they were saying were being echoed in the wider South Africa, through the first hearings of the Truth and Reconciliation Commission. I'll say more about that in a minute: but before I do, a few stories.

Here is the first: South Africa in the early 1980s. The resistance in the country (what the ANC called "the making of the country ungovernable") is reaching its height. The townships are in rebellion. A friend of mine, a cameraman, is in South Africa to make a documentary on the uprisings. He's at a white (remember that in the old South Africa all social events were colour coded) barbecue (*braai*, in South African parlance) when, happening to look up in the direction of Soweto, he saw black plumes of smoke—a tell-tale sign of battles with the police. He wondered out loud what might be going on. But he got no takers in his speculation: for the simple reason that the other guests, looking in exactly the opposite direction, said they didn't know what he was talking about.

My second story: a skip to the South Africa of 1994–1995. I was celebrating Christmas at a friend's house, with about fifteen other people (also all white) when I happened to say something about the soon to be held first hearings of the Truth and Reconciliation Commission (TRC). I wasn't making a particular point, and so I was stunned when my comment was met by a sudden, shocked silence. It was almost as if I said something unbearably rude, my ineptitude covered by another guest's hurried change of topic.

The third story is not so much a story as an observation. In 1994, just before South Africa's election, an exiled writer, Hilda Bernstein, published a book of interviews with a wide range of South African exiles, among them people who had left in the first wave in the 1960s, as well as many who had left later, in the 1970s and 1980s, to join MK. Reading through the five hundred pages of such differing accounts, what came to me most vividly was not so much the pain of exile, but the pain of not being able to express that pain. Here, writ large, it seemed to me, was a manifestation of the "don't mourn, mobilize" phenomenon. People were having to hold to themselves the trauma they experienced, in order that they could work to help end their country's trauma.

And now back to 1995.

Apartheid South Africa is no more, and the Truth and Reconciliation Commission gets going. The moment that many white South Africans (my fellow lunch guests included) have been dreading: the in-your-face confrontation with the past.

Much has been written and said about the TRC, and much of that has, in my opinion, been shot through with wish-fulfilment.

South Africa's transformation is a modern miracle, with its journey from skunk to rainbow nation mirrored by the journey of its most famous citizen, Nelson Mandela, from prisoner to President, from terrorist (at least in some people's eyes) to saint. And, as if this isn't enough, South Africa has displayed to the world the all-feeling, all forgiving, emotional journey that was the TRC.

Excuse my sarcasm: it is only partly intended. I certainly don't mean to decry the miracle.

What took place in South Africa can be thought of as a miracle, and, in its fulfilment, the TRC played a significant part. But I do sometimes find it necessary to remind people about the true origins and purpose of the TRC, which are as follows.

Between 1990, when Nelson Mandela was released from prison, and 1994, the first democratic election, more people died in political violence than in the thirty previous years. The ANC, desperate to put an end to this violence, knew it could only do so by an election that, everybody else knew, it would win. But the then apartheid government refused to allow such an election to take place unless a guarantee was given that its Ministers, its army generals and soldiers, its police generals and ordinary policemen, would not be brought to trial for the things that they had done (many of which were illegal even in apartheid terms). They demanded a generalized indemnity from prosecution.

The ANC would not accept this. What they offered instead was individual amnesty for those who applied for it, and who, in applying, told the truth about what it was that they had done. In addition to these perpetrator hearings, there would be separate victims' hearings: spaces for people to come and, in public, tell the stories of what had happened to them and to their loved ones.

Thus was the TRC born. It was part of a political compromise to end political violence; a voluntary relinquishing of the right to legal justice in exchange for the truth; an attempt to come to terms with the traumas of the past, and then to find a way of moving on; a process full of grand slogans such as "Revealing is healing" and "The truth will set you free".

I don't have the time here to go into the TRC's many ramifications. Suffice it to say that the hearings, and here I am talking about the victims' hearings, were moving and unbearable testimony to the agony of what had gone before. They were relayed, at least in the beginning, in full on TV and, more importantly for a country that was not fully electrified, on radio. A nation was witness to the coming together of people to tell their stories. A reversal in history. They came not to mobilize, but to mourn.

The hearings were hard on the stomach, and hard on the heart, but by the time they were over, I suspect, many who had given testimony (those same people who had experienced so much pain without being able to talk of it) did feel relief. And by the end, even the people like those in the 1980s *braai*, and the 1994 Christmas lunch, would have faced some of what had been done in their name.

The TRC came into being under the auspices of a man, Nelson Mandela, who, having emerged from over a quarter of a century's unjust imprisonment, offered the hand of friendship to his jailors. It was presided over by another man, its chair, Archbishop Desmond Tutu, the head of a Church that has, at is centre, the idea of the redemptive value of forgiveness. But the TRC was not formally meant to be about forgiveness. Forgiveness was certainly prized (and for me, some of the most dubious moments were when relatives of the murdered were encouraged to offer the hand of forgiveness to those who had caused them such great harm). But forgiveness (along with its opposite—perpetrators saying that they were sorry) was a side issue. The architects of the TRC were clear on that. What the TRC was about was reconciliation—thus the name.

And in my view, it was about reconciliation, not between *individuals*, but inside the *society*. Where I think it most succeeded was not by forcing reconciliation between individual victim and perpetrator, between traumatized and those who had caused the trauma, but as the first step in the process of a reconciling the country to an understanding of its terrible past. And on top of that, what the TRC did was help write out the real history of contemporary South Africa. As has often been said, after the TRC, nobody can ever say about South Africa, as some have said about the Holocaust, that it had never happened.

The perpetrator hearings—the original reason for the establishment of a TRC—were very different. Here, judges and lawyers, a supposedly politically balanced panel, sat to consider whether perpetrators had the right to get amnesty. To obtain this, perpetrators had to prove that what they had done had been for a political reason (i.e., you couldn't get amnesty, as one ex-SA policeman tried to, for killing your wife on the grounds that she hated you so much she might have told the ANC what you were up to), that they were telling the truth about it, and that the act was proportional to the intention (for example, if you wanted to get one political activist, you couldn't blow up a nursery of children as well).

Two men, two ex-policemen, applied for amnesty for the murder of my mother, and at the same time, for the murder of another activist, Jeannette Schoon, and her six-year-old daughter Katryn (both of them killed when Jeanette opened an envelope addressed to her). The hearings, which I attended with my two sisters, our intention being to oppose their amnesty applications, brought home to me another dimension of the TRC.

My father had been part of the ANC negotiating committee that had agreed to the compromise of the TRC. At the time, he had known that what this meant was that the men who had killed his wife, our mother, would never be brought to justice for what they had done. What he had said then was that although it was painful to give up the hope of justice, and also the prospect of seeing Ruth's murderers punished, his real revenge would be to force those men to live in a society that they had fought so violently against.

And now my father was dead, and we, his three daughters, had come to witness the application for amnesty of our mother's murderers.

When Ruth died, we knew *what* had killed her. It was the apartheid regime. We had never dreamed, though, that we would one day get to see the who—the real people who had done the deed. And now we found ourselves in the hall of an ugly new-build in Pretoria, watching two men applying for their get-out-of jail-free cards from the new South Africa.

I had met both of them before. The first one, the desk man, I had met when researching my family memoir. I had sat in his office, and listened to his dissociated account of the business he had been involved in—which was the killing of my mother—and I had absorbed his dissociation. I listened to his phrase for murder: "I was in the loop that killed your mother," he said, and then I came out. Feeling nothing. I wrote an account of the meeting in my book— and still mostly without feeling.

I had also met the second man (the explosives expert—old South African speak for bomb maker). As part of a documentary I made to accompany my book, I had door-stepped him in a bed shop in Pretoria where he worked. I had stood, also thinking not much, as he had denied having anything to do with my mother's murder only to, six months later, apply for amnesty for his involvement in her killing.

But to be at a TRC hearing with these men, and in the same room over the weeks that followed, was an entirely different matter.

An amnesty hearing is not like a court of law. There is not much separation between the perpetrators and the people that they have harmed. (In TRC speak, the victims, although this I resist since I think it was my mother who was the real victim of these men.) You end up cheek by jowl with them—using the same parking places, the same coffee queues, the same outside spaces in which to smoke.

I had expected the process to be difficult, but I had not antici-pated how very difficult it would be. And what I hadn't anticipated was that my main difficulty would reside not in the gulf that lay between us, but because of the way I began to understand who these men, these murderers, were. It was impossible not to. We sat in a room with them, eight hours a day. We saw their relatives smil-ing encouragement at them. We heard their excuses. We watched their lawyers laying the ground for their victimhood. The result of this was that I began to feel that I knew how they were thinking, and what they were thinking. In short, I got to know them—and this intimacy, more than anything else, was what was the most difficult thing to endure.

I had also previously believed what they were now trying to con-vince the Commission: that Ruth's killing had been political, and not personal. But now, watching them at such close hand, I began to realize that they had killed for the same reasons that most people kill: out of hatred and out of rage, although in their case theirs was not a moment of loss of control, as many murders are, but a slow-burning, premeditated hatred, not just for my mother, but also for my father and for us, their children; for, in fact, all the white "traitors" who had let down their side. And this hatred still simmered. Because there was no room in their minds to face what they had done—which was to take human life—there was no space either for compassion. They and their lawyers were as bullish, and as attacking even of us, Ruth's daughters, as they would have been in the past.

There are some lessons I draw from being part of this process. The first centres on my own experience of dealing with the trauma. The second is about my writing about such traumas.

To the first. My experience.

I came away from the hearing furious and also furiously upset. I hoped the men would not get amnesty but they did. I do not believe that they should have. I do not believe they killed my mother for a political purpose, and nor do I believe that they had told the truth about what they had done. But I also knew that South Africa wanted to move on. That, by the time of our hearing, the TRC was reaching its sell-by date and that South Africa, as a whole, was far more interested in its present, and its future, than in its past. Only I, and those like me, seemed left behind. And so I came from the hearing upset and angry at what had taken place.

And yet—and it took me some years to understand this—that same, infuriating, upsetting process did actually help me come to terms with the horrors I'd experienced. And the reason is this: what had so upset me was discovering that those murderers (who had not only caused me such great harm, but who had deprived my mother of her life and her chance to see the achievement of everything that she had fought for) were like any other murderers. That they had killed from hatred. And yet they were to get off scot-free, without ever really having to face what they had done. They got their amnesties. The acts they had committed they could, and I'm fairly sure they did, tell themselves wasn't anything to do with murder. It was just politics. That untruth is what so upset me.

But later I was to realize that knowing them, and knowing the truth of their untruth, did help me. I stopped wondering so much about what it was that had happened. I didn't need to—my questions had been answered. Painful as it was, it was better to hear the truth. It's true, that slogan: the truth does set you free.

But now, to writing about this.

Writing about life, especially writing fiction, is not the same thing as living it. A book that just echoes life, that is undigested experience, that seeks to replicate reality rather than explore it, will be an unwieldy, inaccessible thing. But I was set to write a book that was centred on a process that had been so engrossing, and so upsetting, to me.

Before the hearing, I had already decided to set my next book in a fictional amnesty hearing. The intention was not to write about my family, or my mother's death. (I had done that already in my family memoir.) But I already knew that within the process of the TRC were contained many of the ingredients that fuelled my novelist's imagination: the spilling of old secrets, the bringing of the past into the present, the changing of history.

When I set out on a novel, I tend to pre-sell it in outline. For the book that was to become *Red Dust*, I wrote the longest outline I have ever written. Hindsight tells me that I did this because I was trying to convince myself that the story I had decided to tell was one that I actually wanted to tell. Turns out it wasn't. I spent the next six months of writing sequentially throwing out each element of the outline—in effect, un-writing my synopsis—until I ended up with a completely different book.

The book I had planned had been all artifice—a clever plot, carefully plotted out by my rational fiction writer's mind to avoid my own experience. But the impetus, and the feeling, in the book I ended up writing, although it was not about me or about our case, was shot through with my experience in the TRC. This book has two main themes. The first I had known, from the start, I wanted to write about. It was an exploration of whether is it possible for a human being who has been on the receiving end of terrible damage to give up the prospect of legal justice in exchange for the truth (which, of course, poses the question: is it possible to know the truth? Can a perpetrator ever really tell it?).

But the second theme, the one I hadn't known I wanted to write about, sprang from my unexpected experience of the TRC, and that was the way I had grown to know my mother's killers. That made me ask questions about the intimacy between enemies. By coming, against my will, to know those men who had killed my mother, I had to face what it is to live with this knowledge. Out of this was born my decision to write about a torturer and his victim, and that way to explore this intimacy and, indirectly, the complicities between victim and perpetrator.

And I didn't, as often happens in my writing, do this consciously. The story developed from my struggle with the narrative, and with the words that I was laying down. From the set of characters I had started with, I would find that as I wrote myself further into the narrative, the things they did would surprise me. These people who came from me, who were a product of my imagination, also claimed their own existence. One of them was even someone who I, as writer, not only despised, but also grew to actively dislike. I would go as far as to say that I wrote her with hatred. Imagine, therefore, my surprise, and how disconcerted I was, when the first readers kept telling me how much they liked this person.

That, it seems to me, is part of the essence of writing: that the power in a story can lie, not in an attempt to tell others the right or wrong way to solve a problem, but in the willingness to engage with such difficult, even traumatic, issues, without trying to control them.

Red Dust was a technically demanding book, not only because of the complexity of the story but also because in it are a number of characters who, because of who they are, can never meet. The challenge was to lead readers through a series of different story lines and experiences without making them feel as if they were continually starting a new book. It was a challenge, I think, that is also inherent in fictionalizing a process as complex as the TRC. And not only in fictionalizing it. It seems to me no accident that Antjie Krog, who wrote the wonderful non-fiction account of the TRC, *Country of my Skull*, added a fictional element in order to explore emotional aspects of that process that simple reportage could not deliver.

Red Dust eventually also became a film, and the process of distillation from novel to movie was fascinating. I had written a book about the complexity of the TRC. But one thing that can be said about the cinema, powerful though it may be, is that it is also a

simplifying medium. In the book, I took my characters on journeys
at the end of which was not necessarily the happy rainbow nation.
In asking myself the question: is it possible for damaged people to
give up on their right for legal justice?, my answer hadn't always
been a yes. In asking the question: what is it like for a victim of
torture to face their torturer and watch them getting off, scot-free?,
my story had reached the uneasy conclusion that it was not always
easy to move away from such terrible damage.

But the film of *Red Dust* turned out to be a much more optimistic
product. It was a film about the pain of the past, and about the
miracle of the TRC. A good film, I think, and a translation on to the
screen that could find funding even if I might look at it and think,
no, it's not that simple, or, no, I don't agree with that.

But that, it seems to me, is what is wonderful about working in
the medium of fiction. If you were to watch *Red Dust*, the film, without reference to the book, you might believe that my experience of
my trauma in South Africa had led me to the simple endorsement
of the idea of reconciliation and repair that closes the film, whereas
the question I had actually explored was whether damage may not
be too persistent to be simply disappeared in this way. The book is
much darker than the film. For me the film is shot through with the
desire that South Africa fulfils for the world—that there is a better,
nicer, and more humane way of dealing with deadly conflict. And
the paradox is that, although I resist the clichés and wish fulfilment,
I know that South Africa has actually shown that this is true, even
if the process is nowhere near as simple, or as short-term, as people
would want it to be. You only have to look at the crime statistics in
South Africa, and in particular the crimes of violence, to understand
this.

Researching *Red Dust* took me into a part of that country that
was new to me. This was deliberate. I had already written out the
bits of my own life, and my family's life. Now I was set on writing
fiction. I didn't want anybody to be able to point a finger, and say,
there, you see, that's part of her past and therefore it must be her
story. I put a pin, quite literally, into a map of South Africa, and that
way chose the eastern Cape as the place in which to locate my
fictional town of Smitsrivier.

But even if the town were to be fictional, I (a writer increasingly
attracted to big geographical and political landscapes) felt I needed

to root myself in a real landscape. So, for a few weeks, I journeyed through the eastern Cape, drinking in the feel of it. My random choice turned out to be awe-inspiring. I travelled through that grand, almost primeval landscape dominated by mountains whose tops have been imprinted by the outline of the waves that once flowed over what is now a semi-desert. I stayed in small towns that history seemed to have passed by. I spent my time wondering what it must be like to live in one of these towns, which seem so unchanged and unchanging, and then to suddenly find yourself swept up in one of history's grand reversals.

One of the towns I visited was Cradock. Cradock is the birth-place of the ANC, and has long been a home to activists. During the 1980s it was the site of not only much resistance, but also of some of the most barbaric acts of the then security forces. Gideon Niewoudt, the man who applied for amnesty for the murder of Steve Biko (and, incidentally, didn't get it) was based in that area. And in the 1980s, four Cradock-based activists were pulled out of their cars and deliberately and brutally murdered by the police.

Their graves are in the township burial ground, and I wanted to go and pay my respects. So I asked somebody if they could take me there. What I ended up getting was a whole delegation: members of the local ANC, of its youth branch, its women's branch, its trade union branch—fifteen or so people who took me to the graveside, and then afterwards came back with me to my hotel to drink tea.

As we were sitting round, I asked them what they thought of the TRC. "What do you mean?" they said. I asked, "Is it so easy to forgive?" To which their answer came: "We can forgive," they said, "but we will never forget."

It is a phrase frequently repeated in South Africa, and for this reason, it has stayed with me. But it stayed, too, because it is a phrase I find difficult to believe. Forgiveness, it seems to me, is a complex business, especially when the people we are being asked to forgive have no understanding of the harm that they have done. Forgiveness, it also seems, is like making the victim continue to do all the work.

And as for forgetting. Well, I agree, we should not forget. Some of my own work stands as partial testimony to what has gone before. But sometimes a proscription-breaking question infiltrates my mind: is it not relieving, not only for an individual, but also a society, to partially forget?

Take, for example, the literal "born frees". They are kids growing up in a different world (and how thankful we are that they can). They are adults whose lives are not going to be constrained by apartheid. How can they not, somehow, forget? And how can we say that they shouldn't? How can we expect that they must continue to carry our memories of pain? Because, if they do, how do we know that these very memories will not drive them to re-enact the past?

But if, on the other hand, they forget, and if society forgets, who will be there to celebrate the heroism and the sacrifices of those who built a world that would make such forgetting a possibility?

There is loss involved, even in "freedom". Being a born free has taken on a double meaning in South Africa: not just as a literal description of those who came to adulthood in the new South Africa, but as a phrase to mock the new generation that values economic success, and the ability to purchase in the market place, above the ideals of justice and change that inspired their parents.

And now back to the place where I began this talk. The Sea Point supermarket. As I rolled my trolley away from the dried fruit section, I heard one of the ladies saying to my retreating back, "Shame." I think I know what she meant. Shame is a South African–English linguistic quirk. A catch-all, that can be used in many situations to express sympathy, or disapproval, or mere acknowledgement that something has been said or happened. So: "I've hurt my finger" can provoke the response, "Shame". Or, "My father just died" might yield an "Ag shame". Or, as in the super-market, "Shame" probably meant "What a sorry kind of woman is that walking away from us."

How interesting, though, that South Africa has incorporated shame so thoroughly into its lexicon. It was a word that was given a constant outing during the amnesty hearings. The lawyer who acted for us, George Bizos, a household name and hero for his public outing, even in the apartheid years, of police brutality (and, incidentally, a man who was first radicalized in the 1950s by my mother), asked many times of these men applying for amnesty: have you no shame? A good question, that never really got an answer. And how could it? How could men who hadn't ever really faced what they had done face their shame?

Perhaps, again, here was the TRC acting not on individual perpetrators but on the country as whole. Perhaps the shame that was really being addressed was the shame white South Africa might feel at its past refusal to see what was being done in its name, and the shame black South Africa might feel at being so victimized.

Postscript

I have written four books set in South Africa. The first two, pre-liberation, were an examination of issues of heroism and betrayal. The third, my family saga, was another look at heroism, but in this case, the focus was also about the costs of heroism. And then came *Red Dust*—my look at what happens when the past collides with the future, and when the world is no longer just black and white. The books after *Red Dust* have not been set in South Africa, and it is possible that I will never return to the country as a site for my future fictions.

There is no doubt that South Africa, in its horror and its magnificence, is part of the well from which my creativity springs. But what I have learned is that even if I want to write of all these things, I do not have to site my fiction in that country. For what a writer is allowed to do is to use explorations of her own experience and imagination to shine a light, not just on a particular place, or a particular set of circumstances, but on what it is to be human.

Surviving the care system: a story of abandonment and reconnection

Chris Purnell

W hen I was invited to speak at this conference on "Attachment and Trauma" about my own experiences of surviving in the care system, my initial thought was that I do not have anything sufficiently traumatic to talk about. What on earth was I going to say that would be sufficiently interesting or significant to address a conference?

When I thought about it further I realized that my initial response was reminiscent of years ago—when I used to tell people that I spent thirteen of the first sixteen years of my life in institutional care, the usual response was, *that must have been awful for you*, to which I would counter, *well it wasn't as bad for me as it was for some of the kids that I grew up with.*

Of course, I realized later on that this was complete nonsense. It was just as bad for me as it was for any of my peers. My distancing of myself from anything that suggested a traumatic experience was simply part of the strategy that I developed to survive in the system. In attachment terms, it might be understood as an avoidant or dismissing strategy. Many of the kids that I grew up with adopted it; it's the way that we managed to survive long-term in the institutional care system.

The scenes on the film clip show the place where I lived during those thirteen years in care. What you see is, of course, rehearsed for the camera. The two children who played the roles of the brother and sister going into care were actors in a promotional film made by the charity that had guardianship over me.

There is a scene in the film clip, lasting for just a few seconds, where a group of us are playing on a slide and a roundabout in a playground. When I saw the footage originally, I thought we looked like a relatively normal group of kids playing, but then I slowed the tape down and took a closer look at us, frame by frame, and realized the extent to which we too—even as film extras—were playing to the camera. These images are taken from individual frames of film; they are blurred because of the movement of the roundabout and the age of the film, but I think that the expressions on our faces convey a different story from the one intended in the film. Where is the laughter and happiness that the scene is supposed to portray? The few smiles that I see are mask-like. When I look at our faces I see mainly sadness, but there is also angry defiance in some of the stares that meet the intruding of the eye of the camera lens. These moments that are frozen in time convey to me the reality of life in the care system for a group of children whose attachment bonds are either disrupted or altogether broken.

I suppose that some might regard us as simply institutionalized. When I looked up what this meant in the dictionary, it said, *as a result of confinement, to cause to become apathetic and dependent on routine.* This is probably more of an outsider's view of the effects that living in an institution has upon the inmate. Erving Goffman, in his 1960s classic sociological study of life in total institutions (Goffman, 1968), identified a whole range of strategies that inmates adopt in order to survive in the world of the institution, and while he acknowledged that children in orphanages are likely to differ in that very often they had little, if any, experience of life outside of an institutional setting, I think that there are many similarities in what he describes and the strategies that we developed. I remember coming across Goffman's work as a sociology student in the 1970s. It was the first time that I had come across any written account that began to explain to me how I got through the experience of being in care. His work appealed to me because of its emphasis upon survival strategies—pragmatic responses to the situation rather than simply the passive acceptance of an institutional way of life.

In the whole thirteen years of institutional care, I don't recall any conversation with an adult explaining to me exactly why it was that I was living in a children's home, and why it was that I had no identifiable family whatsoever. Interestingly, as kids in care, it wasn't something that I can recall we even discussed with each other in any great detail. It was as though all our effort and energy went into surviving in the system. There was no place for open protest, mourning, or anything else that might distract from the task of simply surviving.

Bessel van der Kolk's chapter on "Developmental trauma disorder" (2008, this volume) describes how children learn to ignore either what they feel or what they perceive in response to the trauma that they have been exposed to, and this I feel resonates strongly with Pat Crittenden's dynamic maturational model of attachment (Crittenden, 2000), which describes the ways in which non-secure children and adults organize their attachment relationships with a bias towards either cognition, ignoring affect, or vice versa. As the paper states, many problems of traumatized children can be understood as efforts to minimize objective threat and regulate emotional distress, and unless care-givers understand the re-enactments, they are likely to label a child, because of his or her behaviour, oppositional; rebellious; antisocial. The care system that I knew didn't tolerate such behaviours.

Being an independent charity, the organization caring for me was able to be selective in terms of who it admitted through its doors. My mother had to apply to have me taken into their care, and her application was vetted by a committee. It is clear, in looking at my records from the time, that she was judged as "a decent sort of girl from a respectable home background"; those who could not be moulded to the institution's ways did not get admitted. I guess that as a baby of just a few months old, the clay of my development was still sufficiently malleable to be readily shaped to fit into the ways of the institution.

There were some children who didn't adapt in the way that most of us did, but in many ways they didn't survive in the system, because the system would not tolerate them. If they couldn't adapt, they were likely to be removed from the system, possibly to end up in more restrictive and controlling institutional settings or secure units. These were the kids who were more *obviously* "troubled". I ran with some of them for a while, and got involved in the fringes of shop-lifting gangs and protection rackets at primary school. We invariably got caught and punished, and, not being as street-wise as some of my peers (most of whom had relatively recent experience of life outside of an institution), I eventually learned that the best way to survive was to adapt to the system rather than fight it.

I think that it is important here just to say something about the plight of the compliant child, the traumatized child who doesn't get noticed through rebellious or antisocial behaviour. In fact, he is likely to go unnoticed because he blends in so readily. If he does get noticed it is because of his adult, "mature" behaviour—the sort that adults are likely to approve of. This is the child who has mastered the skill of ignoring affect; the child that is more likely to be overlooked by carers because he *doesn't* present them with challenging behaviours. I think that, for some professionals who take an interest in the subject, he perhaps might represent the less "interesting" end of a spectrum of solutions to trauma, because he will not present with anything dramatic or confrontational to work with, and his dissociative strategies, if he has them, will be well concealed

My hope is that during this conference, when we talk about working with the impact of trauma, we don't overlook or ignore the traumatized child or adult who adapts in this way. If we do, then all we are doing is simply reinforcing the power of a strategy for surviving danger that depends upon not drawing attention to inner distress through the expression of affect.

I also want to acknowledge that this account of the care system is my individual experience. Some of my peers from that time would differ in some of their views of it. There are some who are grateful to a care system that rescued them from the social deprivation and abuse that they had known earlier. Others still idealize the life in the institution with memories and reminiscences that I personally find difficult to identify with, but I can still respect their view because I know that this is how they make sense of their individual trauma of separation, loss, and deprivation of attachment ties.

Recently, I learned that the care system these days employs advocates to work alongside children in care, to support and represent their interests when dealing with the care professionals who make crucial decisions about their needs and their future. This is such an enlightened initiative.

When I was about ten years old, I remember being summoned to the office of the governor of The Home. His office was located in a clock tower that overlooked the grounds of the entire Home, and I remember climbing the wooden staircase that led to his door, full of trepidation—kids didn't generally get summoned to his office unless they had done something wrong and were about to get the cane. When I arrived at his door he called me in and had me sit on a chair in front of what seemed like an enormous desk. He then informed me that there was a couple who were interested in me and he asked whether I would like to be adopted. I sat there, scared, overawed, and entirely unable to respond, and so he told me to go away and think about it and to let him know.

I didn't know what to think—it was like having the doors of a dark prison suddenly flung open, and being drawn to the light outside, but feeling too afraid to step through the door because the light is too bright and disorientating. Apart from other children, all of whom were equally dazzled by the very idea of being wanted by someone, there was no one to talk to about it. That might at least have given me the possibility of being able to step into the light, as part of me longed to do.

I was too afraid to climb that staircase and go back to the governor to ask any questions; in fact, I was too scared to go back to him at all, and so I never heard anything more about the matter. I lost the opportunity to experience what could probably have been an ordinary family life, and sometimes I wonder what my life would have been like subsequently had I had an advocate to guide and represent me at that time.

So, how did I come to be in the care system to begin with?

I was given up by my mother, a single parent, a few months after my birth, when she placed me in the care of a big national childcare charity. They, in turn, placed me with a foster carer—with someone whom I later came to know as my aunt. I stayed with her for the best part of two years, and I believe that it is largely thanks to her that I survived the following thirteen years. We know that, in terms of security of attachment, the first two years of a child's life are tremen-dously important, and I am convinced that it was my aunt who, in terms of resilience, equipped me to deal with what was to follow.

She maintained contact with my mother, who visited me from time to time, and eventually she began to talk to my mother about the possibility of adopting me. Unfortunately, the charity got wind of what she was attempting to do and accused her of trying to "poach" one of their children. They promptly removed me from the home that I had known for more than two years, saying that my mother had signed an agreement placing me in their care until the age of sixteen.

Not only did they remove me from my home with my aunt, they moved me to an institution 150 miles away, and because my aunt had made moves to take legal action against them, they effectively severed the attachment bond that existed between us by concealing my whereabouts from her. For the next thirteen years she was allowed to write letters to me via the head office of the charity; she did so regularly, and sent me birthday cards. I never received any letters, only the cards. Naturally, as I grew older, I had no memory of her, and when I received the cards I asked who she was. Nobody would ever speak to me about this mysterious person.

Thus began my life in institutional care. I have no idea how quickly I settled into this new life—as I grew older, it was all that I knew. The Home was built as a village, with about thirteen houses, each containing around twelve to fifteen children. Each house was run by women known to us as "Sisters". My memory of the Sister who was in charge of the house that I lived in is that of a cold, distant woman who had dark moods that I found incredibly threat-ening. She wasn't the sort of person with whom any child could form a secure attachment.

Usually, when we think about attachment, we do so in the context of care-giving relationships. Where care-givers fail to provide us with adequate safety and security, we are usually left with one or other of two difficulties. The first is how to elicit comfort from care-givers who routinely withhold their care-giving responses, and the second is how to predict inconsistencies or perhaps danger in the responses of care-givers.

My experience of the care system was that it *was* predictable and it *was* consistent—it routinely denied us access to the sense of safety and comfort that any child needs. I was fed, clothed, and sheltered, but there was no significant care-giver with whom I was able to develop a secure attachment. There was no love. I think that what most of us did to survive in that institution was to develop strategies to deal with danger in the absence of care-giving, rather than to maintain proximity to a care-giver.

I learned to deal with danger in a particular way, and I would like to read to you a passage from a manuscript that illustrates this.

Sister Jane was a small, grey haired woman with a sharp tongue and cold, steel grey-blue eyes that were framed with wired rimmed spectacles. She had dark moods that the little boy could read so clearly and which filled him with dread. Why she should make him feel so uneasy was unclear, but being in her presence was like being in close proximity to a bomb that might explode at any moment and he had to do what ever he could to try and defuse it.

That evening after tea, all of the children had been playing a game of hide and seek around the house. The little boy had played too; he had hidden in the dining room under the table that was still covered with the blue and white striped cloth that had been used during teatime, the edges of which hung down almost to the floor concealing him from view. His bare knees felt cold against the quarry tile floor, which was littered with the food debris dropped from the plates of a dozen hungry children.

As he crouched in his hiding place he could hear shrieks and squeals of excitement as someone was discovered hiding in the playroom next door. Suddenly Sister Jane entered the dining room and for the little boy, the ticking of the bomb started, becoming deafening in his ears and all but drowning out the noise from the next room. He hastily scrambled out from under the table, heart pounding and his mind frantically searching for ways to prevent what felt like an imminent explosion that could be triggered by those shrieks of laughter in the next room.

Sister Jane's cold gaze pierced into him as he emerged from under the cloth. He feared that she would hear his heart pounding like a drum within his chest as he tried to ignore the gaze as best he could. He attempted to distract himself from the feared explosion and helped to clear away the dirty crockery. "Can I help you with the clearing up please Sister?" he heard himself say. Sister Jane nodded in consent, her thin, tight lips remaining silent as her gaze returned to attend to the task in hand. Being helpful might distract her from the noise of play in the next room. As he gathered up the plates and cups, the loud ticking faded into the background, to be replaced by the shrieks of laughter that continued to emanate from the playroom as the rest of the children continued the game, oblivious to the danger that he had averted by defusing the bomb.

It was only fear that prevented him from being fully aware of just how much he hated this woman for the cold and distant manner that contributed so much to his inner loneliness. She had her favourites and he knew that he wasn't one of them, although she wasn't openly hostile towards him. He had witnessed her hostility towards some of the older children who were probably not as skilled as he was at pre-empting any attack by reading and defusing her deadly moods with compliant helpfulness.

This woman represents a description of my main care provider and she terrified me. I think that the only way that I was able to survive in her care was to not show fear and to be well behaved. I don't think I did this to gain approval so much as to avoid attack. Her care-giving was not sufficient to protect me from the abuse that took place in The Home.

It is only a matter of time before a child who is desperately lonely and emotionally vulnerable in this environment becomes the target for sexual abuse, and this is what happened to me. The perpetrator wasn't a member of staff; he was an adolescent boy. I was five or six years old and desperately in need of love and attention. He gave me the attention that I needed, and a great deal more that I didn't ask for, want, or understand. Although I didn't like what he did to me I had no way of making it stop. There was no one to turn to. That boy was just as much a victim as I was of a care system that was ignorant about the attachment needs of children.

There isn't time to recount everything that happened during those years—not that I can remember it all of course—but the thing that I take some pride in when I look back is my resilience. I do remember feeling so desperately alone when I was seven or eight years old that I simply wanted to die. No one had any idea that I felt this way; you survive in the system by not showing any sign of distress or trauma, but on the inside I was desperately unhappy. The only obstacle between me and suicide was knowledge: at that age I had absolutely no idea of how I might make myself die, how I might kill myself. John Bowlby (1975) described a process of protest, despair, and detachment that children go through when faced with prolonged separation. He saw this as a childhood form of depression. What I remember is that for me the detachment was simply a mask to conceal an intense inner feeling of despair that was never displaced.

Being part of a Christian charity, life in The Home had a strong religious element. We had to go to chapel every morning before going to school, where we then had religious assembly, and on Saturdays we still had chapel. On Sundays it was chapel in the morning, Sunday school in the afternoon, and chapel again in the evening, when we mindlessly chanted prayers and hymns and listened to what seemed like endless sermons. I remember hating God; I remember thinking if he was an all powerful father who looked after all of his children like they said, why had he abandoned me in that place? I couldn't understand what I might have done to deserve such a punishment.

They taught us to sing songs about Jesus loving us. They told us that he loved children all over the world—white, red, yellow, brown, and black. If this was the case, then why did he allow the children at school to taunt me because of the colour of my skin? There were no Black adult role models in The Home to talk to me about these things; I daresay that no one ever considered that it might be important, and when faced with this sort of situation, the hatred that you experience inevitably gets turned inward and you end up hating yourself.

Throughout these years I sustained myself with the fantasy of an idealized mother who would come and rescue me. She was out there somewhere trying to find me, and one day she would come for me. I built a picture in my mind of what she looked like, and I even dreamed about her.

Nobody had any idea of just how traumatized I was by my experience in care. I hardly knew it myself. They only saw the outer shell. The polite and well-behaved child, who made himself like-able through his quiet disposition.

Pat Crittenden (2000) describes trauma as the psychological responses that we make to dangerous events. She identifies the experience of, and responses to, danger as the primary influence in shaping attachment patterns as an additional factor to the emphasis upon the experience of a secure base. As a child in care, there was no secure base, and potential danger lay at every turn; in response you learn *not* to show what you truly feel, you *never* say what you think when it is likely to conflict or disagree the with adults who hold power over you, and you *always* remain attentive to the adults who hold that power. My response to all of these dangers was also to search inside myself for safety.

I developed what I later came to identify as that which Winnicott (1984) described as a false self. I allowed myself to depend upon no one—in the absence of any external secure base, my safe place was inside of me. If you are teased, put down, and ridiculed enough for showing distress through crying, you learn eventually not to cry, and then you lose the ability. As a small child I remember that I used to very quietly sing to myself and rock myself to sleep at night. I guess that this was just one of my strategies for self-regulating affect. I remember it was comforting, and it probably gave me a greater internal sense of safety, but it also prompted teasing and ridicule from other children and therefore became something shameful that had to be controlled.

Judith Herman, in her book *Trauma and Recovery* (1992), identifies three stages to the process of recovery from complex trauma: creating safety, mourning, and reconnection. Safety has to come first, and, as I say, I created this inside myself. I built a fortress, but it was just as effective in locking me in as it was at shutting the world out.

The first tentative steps that I took towards any experience of external safety—or a secure base—that I can recall was when I left The Home at the age of sixteen, and was fortunate enough to go and live with a foster mother who fostered because she loved kids. She was the first person I can remember ever telling me that she loved me. I had no idea how to respond to her; she might as well have been speaking Martian, but she kept on telling me anyway. I do remember that by the age of eighteen I was able to respond to her telling me "I love you" with a rather stiff and gruff "well you're not bad yourself, either". I don't think that she ever knew just how important she was in helping me to change, and I wasn't able to tell her during her lifetime.

During this time I also re-found my aunt. When I left the Home I asked them to tell me who this mysterious "auntie" was, and they gave me her last known address. I wrote to her and we were reunited. Thus, the process of reconnection that Herman talks about began. But, of course, it isn't possible to reconnect without mourning the losses relating to the original trauma.

My aunt was the only living connection that I had with my mother, and it is hard to begin to describe just how important this was to me. I hungered for every snippet of information about her that might help me gain a sense of what she was like, and I felt an increasing anger with the institution that had deprived me of so much. They had denied me the opportunity of a secure home with someone who really did love and care for me; they severed the tenuous contact that I had with my mother by moving me 150 miles away from her. (In the mid 1950s a 300-mile round trip for a few hours of contact wasn't something that most people would find possible, and in my mother's case, as I later discovered, she would have to explain where she was going to a family who weren't even aware of my existence.) But the thing that I found the most unforgivable was that in severing these links they stripped me of any sense of identity. I had no history and no idea of who I was. The more aware I became of how unnecessary the thirteen years in care had been, the angrier I felt.

People who knew about my background at that time suggested that I might want to go and work with children in care as a career. I knew that the experience was too raw and too unresolved for me to be able to work within the care system. I opted for youth work instead, and was drawn to working with troubled and disaffected young people. I felt that in doing this I was transforming a negative experience into something positive.

I loved working with young people because for the most part they were refreshingly open in what they thought and what they felt—something that I admired because of my own restrictive experience. If they didn't like you they'd let you know it, but if you were able to make a connection with them they'd make use of it; in some instances these connections that we made provided them with the sort of life-line that no one ever offered to me.

I developed specialist areas of interest in youth work, which involved challenging young people to think about and explore their attitudes and feelings towards each other and about their lives generally. It was exciting work, but the shock came when I realized that unconsciously I was challenging young people to deal with issues that I hadn't anywhere near resolved for myself!

Around about this time, both my foster mother and my aunt died within about six months of each other, and I hit a crisis that I didn't know how to deal with emotionally. I became acutely aware of the discrepancy between the solid, secure exterior that I presented to the world and feelings that I held inside that didn't feel secure; they felt distinctly crumbly. I found it increasingly hard to identify with the calm, mature, and balanced adult that others perceived me as. I felt distinctly the opposite inside, and I didn't know which was the real me any more.

You could say that my false self was having an identity crisis. This is the problem with a self that is constructed in this way; it isn't flexible. It is designed for a specific purpose and isn't equipped to cope with an earthquake of change. And because it doesn't have flexibility and cannot adapt to massive life-changing events, it has difficulty in continuing to function, but rather than simply reject this aspect of the self as dysfunctional, we need to honour it because we wouldn't have survived without it. I have lost count of the number of my psychotherapy clients that I have subsequently explained this to. It is not something that I learned from a textbook, although I know that there are plenty of references available.

The next stage of my recovery involved a journey of self-discovery on a two-year humanistic facilitator training course. When I started the training I believed that it was to help me to improve my ability to facilitate youth work groups. It turned into something else as I was confronted with aspects of myself that I hadn't even considered existed. A particularly memorable event (for all of the wrong reasons) was one residential weekend when the dam burst on all of those years of bottled-up trauma. I spent the best part of two days in floods of tears that I couldn't control. It was probably the first time that I had really cried in more than twenty years, and I couldn't explain exactly why it was that I was crying. Not because I couldn't think of a reason, but because there were too many reasons. It all came out in one huge cathartic deluge, and I only really began make sense of it all when I later started my own personal therapy and my psychotherapy training.

This was when I came across ideas and concepts that were new to me: the "true self"—how would I ever know what was truly me?

People around me were talking about their "inner child"—what on earth did they mean? Did I really have one? If so where was he?

The other important thread that was simultaneously contributing to the process of recovery for me was the birth of my sons. They played an important role in helping me to reconnect with myself. I always have found it difficult to put into words the experience of that reconnection. The closest that I can get to describing it is to compare it with what Daniel Stern (2004), describes as "moments of meeting"; those moments of experience with another person that fundamentally change the intersubjective relationship between the two of you. Moments that don't necessarily have words to express or describe them. It was like meeting myself as a small child through a moment of meeting with another small child, but the strangest part of the experience for me was that I was meeting my true child self for the first time. It conjured up powerful mental images of myself as a child in The Home, but now I was able to stand outside of myself and for the first time to appreciate the innocence of that child. It was a deeply profound experience, and it happened many times subsequently.

It was these moments that helped to guide me in negotiating the maze of fatherhood. Never having had the experience of a relationship with a father (good or bad), this has been one of the biggest challenges, but it isn't an impossible task if you are prepared to allow your children to guide you, and you are able to recognize the hurt inside yourself and not project too many of your fears, insecurities, and needs on to them. It also helps to have a partner who is able to model an alternative to your own restricted experiences.

The final major part of my process of recovery was when I finally found my mother. It was thirty-five years after I went into care, and the process through which I found her was quite remarkable, but that is another story in itself. One of the stranger parts of the experience was our first reunion meeting—when I first saw her it was a shock. I went to her house to meet her, having first made contact by telephone. She came to the door and that's when I realized that in my mind I still held an image of her that I had created years earlier in dreams and fantasies as a child. The shock was being confronted with a woman who was in her late fifties, when in my mind I still had the childhood idealized image of the young woman who had given up her child.

The process of reconnecting became more complex from here in. The image of idealized mother was shattered, and the process began of coming to terms with her role in my abandonment and subsequent trauma. I discovered a mother who was not capable of offering the sort of idealized attachment relationship that I had clung on to and hoped for over the years.

She, too, had had her own traumas over the years, which I later discovered had led her down the road to alcoholism, which ultimately destroyed her. We had a relationship that lasted for nine years. There were some good times, but also it was a painful and difficult time. My need to reconnect meant that I had what felt like a million and one questions that needed answers, many of which were too painful or too difficult for her to answer. She coped with her own trauma by using what I came to think of as selective amnesia—some things were simply blocked out. They weren't actually forgotten, but they were far too difficult to remember and talk about.

Of course, no amount of psychotherapeutic insight or skill can adequately equip you to deal with a relationship with someone close who has lost the will to live and is passively destroying themselves through alcoholic neglect. I felt cheated and angry at the time, but I also learned a great deal about myself and about alcoholism and its effect upon families and relationships, and I do think that much of what I learned has had an impact upon how I work.

I'm not suggesting that life experiences in themselves are any sort of qualification, but knowing what it is actually like to feel the flatness and emptiness of a deep depression, or the intense fear or anxiety of an affective state that you don't have any control over, can contribute a great deal to your ability to really understand and connect with your clients. Provided, of course, you've had the opportunity to work through these difficulties in your own therapy.

Some people will instinctively know that you have personal experience of trauma simply through some of the moments of meeting in the psychotherapeutic relationship. In other instances they don't pick it up and they tell you that you can't begin to imagine what it was like to experience their particular trauma, and sometimes this is true. At other times you just have to say nothing, but allow yourself to be guided by your own inner experience.

You can use your own woundedness to work psychotherapeutically with trauma, but you have to be able hold it as countertransference and use it as a personal reference point to help you to understand rather than allow it to impinge upon the relationship. Sometimes that isn't easy and sometimes it isn't possible.

I recently found this while working with an asylum seeker who was trying to come to terms with the traumatic impact of the forced severance of her attachments to her home country and her family. In one particular session she became very distressed, and at one point she asked me whether I could possibly imagine what it was like to be cut off from one's family and to be so afraid and all alone. I heard myself replying in the affirmative. It wasn't a measured response, it was a "now moment". It was a moment where, as Stern (2004) puts it, authenticity takes over from the technical moves of intervention. She gave me a surprised and questioning look, and I attempted to retrieve the technical stance by simply saying that I had been separated from my family for many years but that eventually we had been reunited. I didn't need to say any more than this, and she didn't appear to feel the need to ask. The "moment of meeting" that came out of this "now moment" created an important shift in our therapeutic relationship, as we discovered a new unspoken, intersubjective understanding of loss and grief.

Loss of contact with home and family is traumatic in many ways. One important aspect of reconnection for me has been the discovery—at least in part—of who I am. This is the only photograph that I possess of myself as a child in The Home (see Photo 1).

Photo 1.

Photo 2.

When a child starts life with no identity other than a name, you can more or less guarantee that he is going reach a stage where he will begin to lose touch with who he is because he has no history.

Although some of my history is irretrievably lost, I have been fortunate enough to regain a substantial part of it in the form of photographs and artefacts, and this has been tremendously important. To hold in your hands the war medals of a grandfather who you never met during his lifetime is a truly powerful experience. The people in the photograph (see Photo 2) are my family. Most of them are now dead—some of them I did meet, but even those who died before I was born or before I was able to find this history, still give me a powerful sense of who I am. I feel as though I know them. There are some who I believe are still alive, but I have yet to trace them. Perhaps one day I will find them, or perhaps my children will, and so the process of reconnection will continue.

Until recently I never imagined that I would ever stand in front of an audience and recount my story in this way. It is contrary to everything that I learned to do in order to survive in institutional care; to be the focus of attention rather than to blend in and not be noticed; to acknowledge the existence of emotional needs and feelings that it was dangerous to have; and, as I stated at the beginning, part of me never really imagined that there was even a story to tell that anyone might want to listen to. Even now the ghosts from my past still whisper, "You're just feeling sorry for yourself! It could have been far worse!" But that is precisely why it is so important for me to be standing here speaking to you, and so for this reason, if no other, I thank you for listening.

References

Bowlby, J. (1975). *Attachment and Loss: Volume 2. Separation, Anxiety and Anger*. Harmondsworth: Pelican.

Crittenden, P. M. (2000). A dynamic–maturational approach to continuity and change in patterns of attachment. In: P. M. Crittenden & A. H. Claussen (Eds.), *The Organisation of Attachment Relationships—Maturation, Culture and Context*. New York: Cambridge University Press.

Goffman, E. (1968). *Asylums: Essays on the Social Situation of Mental Patients and other Inmates*. Harmondsworth: Pelican.

Herman, J. L. (1992). *Trauma and Recovery: The Aftermath of Violence—From Domestic Abuse to Political Terror.* New York: Basic Books.

Stern, D. N. (2004). *The Present Moment in Psychotherapy and Everyday Life.* London: W. W. Norton.

van der Kolk, B. A. (2008). Developmental trauma disorder: towards a rational diagnosis for children with complex trauma histories. In: S. Benamer & K. White (Eds.), *Attachment and Trauma.* London: Karnac.

Winnicott, D. W. (1984). *The Maturational Processes and the Facilitating Environment.* London: Karnac.

The John Bowlby Memorial Lecture 2006. Developmental trauma disorder: a new, rational diagnosis for children with complex trauma histories[1]

Bessel van der Kolk

C hildhood trauma, including abuse and neglect, is probably the single most important public health challenge in the USA, a challenge that has the potential to be largely resolved by appropriate prevention and intervention. Each year, more than three million children are reported to authorities for abuse or neglect in the USA; about one million of those cases are substantiated (US Department of Health and Human Services, Administration on Children, Youth and Families, 2003). Many thousands more undergo traumatic medical and surgical procedures and are victims of accidents and of community violence (Spinazzola et al., 2005, p. 433). However, most trauma begins at home; the vast majority of people (about 80%) responsible for child maltreatment are children's own parents.

Inquiry into developmental milestones and family medical history is routine in medical and psychiatric examinations. In contrast, social taboos prevent obtaining information about childhood trauma, abuse, neglect, and other exposures to violence. Research has shown that traumatic childhood experiences not only are extremely common, but also have a profound impact on many different areas of functioning. For example, children exposed to

alcoholic parents or domestic violence rarely have secure child-
hoods; their symptomatology tends to be pervasive and multi-
faceted and is likely to include depression, various medical
illnesses, and a variety of impulsive and self-destructive behaviours. Approaching each of these problems piecemeal, rather than
as expressions of a vast system of internal disorganization, runs the
risk of losing sight of the forest in favour of one tree.

Complex trauma

The traumatic stress field has adopted the term "complex trauma"
to describe the experience of multiple, chronic, and prolonged,
developmentally adverse traumatic events, most often of an interpersonal nature (e.g., sexual or physical abuse, war, community
violence) and early-life onset. These exposures often occur within
the child's care-giving system and include physical, emotional, and
educational neglect and child maltreatment beginning in early
childhood (Cook et al., 2005, p. 390; Spinazzola et al., 2005, p. 433).

In the Adverse Childhood Experiences (ACE) study by Kaiser
Permanente and the Centers for Disease Control and Prevention
(Felitti et al., 1998), 17,337 adult health maintenance organization
(HMO) members responded to a questionnaire about adverse childhood experiences, including childhood abuse, neglect, and family
dysfunction. Eleven per cent reported having been emotionally
abused as a child, 30.1% reported physical abuse, and 19.9% sexual
abuse. In addition, 23.5% reported being exposed to family alcohol
abuse, 18.8% were exposed to mental illness, 12.5% witnessed their
mothers being battered, and 4.9% reported family drug abuse.

The ACE study showed that adverse childhood experiences are
vastly more common than recognized or acknowledged and that
they have a powerful relationship to adult health half a century
later. The study confirmed earlier investigations that found a highly
significant relationship between adverse childhood experiences
and depression, suicide attempts, alcoholism, drug abuse, sexual
promiscuity, domestic violence, cigarette smoking, obesity, physical
inactivity, and sexually transmitted diseases. In addition, the more
adverse childhood experiences reported, the more likely a person

was to develop heart disease, cancer, stroke, diabetes, skeletal fractures, and liver disease.

Isolated traumatic incidents tend to produce discrete, conditioned behavioural and biological responses to reminders of the trauma, such as those captured in the post traumatic stress disorder (PTSD) diagnosis. In contrast, chronic maltreatment or inevitable repeated traumatization, such as occurs in children who are exposed to repeated medical or surgical procedures, have pervasive effects on the development of mind and brain.

Chronic trauma interferes with neurobiological development (Ford, 2005, p. 410) and the capacity to integrate sensory, emotional and cognitive information into a cohesive whole. Developmental trauma sets the stage for unfocused responses to subsequent stress (Cicchetti & Toth, 1995) leading to dramatic increases in the use of medical, correctional, social and mental health services (Drossman et al., 1990). People with childhood histories of trauma, abuse, and neglect make up almost the entire criminal justice population in the USA (Teplin, Abram, McClelland, Dulcan, & Mericle, 2002). Physical abuse and neglect are associated with very high rates of arrest for violent offences. In one prospective study of victims of abuse and neglect, almost half were arrested for non traffic-related offences by age thirty-two (Widom & Maxfield, 1996). Seventy-five per cent of perpetrators of child sexual abuse report that they themselves been sexually abused during childhood (Romano & De Luca, 1997).

These data suggest that most interpersonal trauma on children is perpetuated by victims who grow up to become perpetrators or repeat victims of violence. This tendency to repeat represents an integral aspect of the cycle of violence in our society.

Trauma, care-givers, and affect tolerance

Children learn to regulate their behaviour by anticipating their care-givers' responses to them (Schore, 1994). This interaction allows them to construct what Bowlby called "internal working models" (Bowlby, 1980). A child's internal working models are defined by the internalization of the affective and cognitive characteristics of their primary relationships. Because early experiences occur in the

context of a developing brain, neural development and social interaction are inextricably intertwined. As Don Tucker has said,

> For the human brain, the most important information for success-
> ful development is conveyed by the social rather than the physical
> environment. The baby brain must begin participating effectively in
> the process of social information transmission that offers entry into
> the culture. [Tucker, 1992]

Early patterns of attachment affect the quality of information
processing throughout life (Crittenden, 1992). Secure infants learn
to trust both what they feel and how they understand the world.
This allows them to rely on both their emotions and their thoughts
to react to any given situation. Their experience of feeling understood provides them with the confidence that they are capable of
making good things happen and that, if they do not know how to
deal with difficult situations, they can find people who can help
them find a solution.

Secure children learn a complex vocabulary to describe their
emotions, such as love, hate, pleasure, disgust, and anger. This
allows them to communicate how they feel and to formulate effi-
cient response strategies. They spend more time describing physiological states such as hunger and thirst, as well as emotional states,
than do maltreated children (Cicchetti & White, 1990). Under most
conditions, parents are able to help their distressed children restore
a sense of safety and control. The security of the attachment bond
mitigates against trauma-induced terror. When trauma occurs in the
presence of a supportive, if helpless, care-giver, the child's response
is likely to mimic that of the parent—the more disorganized the
parent, the more disorganized the child (Browne & Finkelhor, 1986).

However, if the distress is overwhelming, or when the care-
givers themselves are the source of the distress, children are unable
to modulate their arousal. This causes a breakdown in their capacity to process, integrate, and categorize what is happening. At the
core of traumatic stress is a breakdown in the capacity to regulate
internal states. If the distress does not ease, the relevant sensations,
affects, and cognitions cannot be associated—they are dissociated
into sensory fragments—and, as a result, these children cannot
comprehend what is happening or devise and execute appropriate
plans of action (van der Kolk & Fisler, 1995).

When care-givers are emotionally absent, inconsistent, frustrat-ing, violent, intrusive, or neglectful, children are likely to become intolerably distressed and unlikely to develop a sense that the external environment is able to provide relief. Thus, children with insecure attachment patterns have trouble relying on others to help them and are unable to regulate their emotional states by them-selves. As a result, they experience excessive anxiety, anger, and longings to be taken care of. These feelings may become so extreme as to precipitate dissociative states or self-defeating aggression. "Spaced out" and hyper aroused children learn to ignore either what they feel (their emotions), or what they perceive (their cogni-tions).

When children are unable to achieve a sense of control and stability, they become helpless. If they are unable to grasp what is going on and unable do anything about it to change it, they go immediately from (fearful) stimulus to (fight/flight/freeze) res-ponse without being able to learn from the experience. Subse-quently, when exposed to reminders of a trauma (e.g., sensations, physiological states, images, sounds, situations), they tend to behave as if they were traumatized all over again—as a catastrophe (Streeck-Fischer & van der Kolk, 2000). Many problems of trauma-tized children can be understood as efforts to minimize objective threat and to regulate their emotional distress (Pynoos et al., 1987). Unless care-givers understand the nature of such re-enactments, they are likely to label the child as "oppositional", "rebellious", "unmotivated", or "antisocial".

The dynamics of childhood trauma

Young children, still embedded in the here-and-now and lacking the capacity to see themselves in the perspective of the larger context, have no choice but to see themselves as the centre of the universe. In their eyes, everything that happens is related directly to their own sensations. Development consists of learning to master and "own" one's experiences and to learn to experience the present as part of one's personal experience over time (Kegan, 1982). Piaget (1954) called this "decentration": moving from being one's reflexes, movements, and sensations to having them.

Predictability and continuity are critical for a child to develop a good sense of causality and learn to categorize experience. A child needs to develop categories to be able to place any particular experience in a larger context. Only then will he or she be able to evaluate what is happening and entertain a range of options with which they can affect the outcome of events. Imagining being able to play an active role leads to problem-focused coping (Streeck-Fischer & van der Kolk, 2000).

mentally [handwritten margin note]

If children are exposed to unmanageable stress, and if the caregiver does not take over the function of modulating the child's arousal, as occurs when children are exposed to family dysfunction or violence, the child will be unable to organize and categorize experiences in a coherent fashion. Unlike adults, children do not have the option to report, move away, or otherwise protect themselves; they depend on their care-givers for their very survival.

When trauma emanates from within the family, children experience a crisis of loyalty and organize their behaviour to survive within their families. Being prevented from articulating what they observe and experience, traumatized children will organize their behaviour around keeping the secret, deal with their helplessness with compliance or defiance, and acclimatize in any way they can to entrapment in abusive or neglectful situations (Piaget, 1954).

When professionals are unaware of children's need to adjust to traumatizing environments and expect that children should behave in accordance with adult standards of self-determination and autonomous, rational choices, these maladaptive behaviours tend to inspire revulsion and rejection. Ignorance of this fact is likely to lead to labelling and stigmatizing children for behaviours that are meant to ensure survival.

Being left to their own devices leaves chronically traumatized children with deficits in emotional self-regulation. This results in problems with self-definition as reflected by a lack of a continuous sense of self, poorly modulated affect and impulse control, including aggression against self and others, and uncertainty about the reliability and predictability of others, expressed as distrust, suspiciousness, and problems with intimacy, resulting in social isolation (Summit, 1983). Chronically traumatized children tend to suffer from distinct alterations in states of consciousness, including amnesia, hypermnesia, dissociation, depersonalization and derealization,

flashbacks and nightmares of specific events, school problems, difficulties in attention regulation, disorientation in time and space, and
sensorimotor developmental disorders. The children often are literally are "out of touch" with their feelings, and often have no
language to describe internal states (Cole & Putnam, 1992).

When a child lacks a sense of predictability, he or she may experience difficulty developing object constancy and inner representa-
tions of their own inner world or their surroundings. As a result,
they lack a good sense of cause and effect and of their own contri- *Bad?*
butions to what happens to them. Without internal maps to guide
them, they act, instead of plan, and show their wishes in their
behaviours, rather than discussing what they want (Streeck-Fischer
& van der Kolk, 2000). Unable to appreciate clearly who they or
others are, they have problems enlisting other people as allies on
their behalf. Other people are sources of terror or pleasure but are
rarely fellow human beings with their own sets of needs and desires.

These children also have difficulty appreciating novelty.
Without a map to compare and contrast, anything new is potentially threatening. What is familiar tends to be experienced as safer,
even if it is a predictable source of terror (Streeck-Fischer & van der
Kolk, 2000). Traumatized children rarely discuss their fears and
traumas spontaneously. They also have little insight into the relationship between what they do, what they feel, and what has
happened to them. They tend to communicate the nature of their
traumatic past by repeating it in the form of interpersonal enact-
ments, both in their play and in their fantasy lives.

Childhood trauma and psychiatric illness

Post traumatic stress disorder (PTSD) is not the most common
psychiatric diagnosis in children with histories of chronic trauma
(Cook et al., 2005, p. 390). For example, in one study of 364 abused
children (Ackerman, Newton, McPherson, Jones, & Dykman, 1998).
The most common diagnoses in order of frequency were separation
anxiety disorder, oppositional defiant disorder, phobic disorders,
PTSD, and ADHD children (*ibid.*). Numerous studies of traumatized
children find problems with unmodulated aggression and impulse
control (Lewis & Shanok, 1979; Steiner, Garcia, & Matthews, 1997),

attentional and dissociative problems (Teicher et al., 2003) and difficulty negotiating relationships with care-givers, peers, and, later in
life, intimate partners (Schneider-Rosen & Cicchetti, 1984). A history
of childhood physical and sexual assault is associated with a host
of other psychiatric diagnoses in adolescence and adulthood.
These may include substance abuse, borderline and antisocial
personality, and eating, dissociative, affective, somatoform, cardio-
vascular, metabolic, immunological, and sexual disorders (van der
Kolk, 2003).

The results of the *Diagnostic and Statistical Manual of Mental
Disorders, Fourth Edition* (*DSM-IV*) Field Trial suggested that trauma
has its most pervasive impact during the first decade of life and
becomes more circumscribed (i.e., more like "pure" PTSD) with age
(van der Kolk, Roth, Pelcovitz, Mandel, & Spinazzola, 2008). The
diagnosis of PTSD is not developmentally sensitive and does not
adequately describe the effect of exposure to childhood trauma on
the developing child. Because infants and children who experience
multiple forms of abuse often experience developmental delays
across a broad spectrum, including cognitive, language, motor, and
socialization skills (Culp, Heide, & Richardson, 1987), they tend to
display very complex disturbances, with a variety of different, often
fluctuating, presentations.

However, because there is currently no other diagnostic entity
that describes the pervasive effects of trauma on child development, these children are given a range of "co-morbid" diagnoses, as
if they occurred independently from the PTSD symptoms. None of
these does justice to the spectrum of problems of traumatized children, and none provides guidelines on what is needed for effective
prevention and intervention. By relegating the full spectrum of
trauma-related problems to seemingly unrelated "co-morbid" conditions, fundamental trauma-related disturbances may be lost to
scientific investigation and clinicians may run the risk of applying
treatment approaches that are not helpful.

A new diagnosis: developmental trauma disorder

The question of how best to organize the very complex emotional,
behavioural, and neurobiological sequelae of childhood trauma has

vexed clinicians for several decades. Because *DSM-IV* includes a diagnosis for adult onset trauma, PTSD, the label often is applied to children as well. However, the majority of traumatized children do not meet the diagnostic criteria for PTSD (Kiser, Heston, Millsap, & Pruitt, 1987; Cook et al., 2005, p.390) and PTSD cannot capture the multiplicity of exposures over critical developmental periods.

Moreover, the PTSD diagnosis does not capture the developmental effects of childhood trauma: the complex disruptions of affect regulation; the disturbed attachment patterns; the rapid behavioural regressions and shifts in emotional states; the loss of autonomous strivings; the aggressive behaviour against self and others; the failure to achieve developmental competencies; the loss of bodily regulation in areas of sleep, food, and self care; the altered schemas of the world; the anticipatory behaviour and traumatic expectations; the multiple somatic problems, from gastrointestinal distress to headaches; the apparent lack of awareness of danger and resulting self endangering behaviours; the self-hatred and self-blame; and the chronic feelings of ineffectiveness.

Interestingly, many forms of interpersonal trauma, in particular psychological maltreatment, neglect, separation from care-givers, traumatic loss, and inappropriate sexual behaviour, do not necessarily meet *DSM-IV*'s "Criterion A" definition for a traumatic event. This criterion requires, in part, an experience involving "actual or threatened death or serious injury, or a threat to the physical integrity of self or others" (American Psychiatric Association, 1994). Children exposed to these common types of interpersonal adversity thus typically would not qualify for a PTSD diagnosis unless they also were exposed to experiences or events that qualify as "traumatic", even if they have symptoms that would otherwise warrant a PTSD diagnosis.

This finding has several implications for the diagnosis and treatment of traumatized children and adolescents. Non Criterion A forms of childhood trauma exposure—such as psychological or emotional abuse and traumatic loss—have been demonstrated to be associated with PTSD symptoms and self-regulatory impairments in children and into adulthood (Basile, Arias, Desai, & Thompson, 2004; Higgins & McCabe, 2000). Thus, classification of traumatic events may need to be defined more broadly, and treatment may need to address directly the sequelae of these interpersonal adversities, given their prevalence and potentially severe negative effects on children's development and emotional health.

The Complex Trauma taskforce of The National Child Traumatic Stress Network has been concerned about the need for a more precise diagnosis for children with complex histories. In an attempt to more clearly delineate what these children suffer from and to serve as a guide for rational therapeutics, this taskforce has started to conceptualize a new diagnosis provisionally called developmental trauma disorder (van der Kolk, 2005, p. 404). This proposed diagnosis is organized around the issue of triggered dysregulation in response to traumatic reminders, stimulus generalization, and the anticipatory organization of behaviour to prevent the recurrence of the trauma effects.

This provisional diagnosis is based on the concept that multiple exposures to interpersonal trauma, such as abandonment, betrayal, physical or sexual assaults, or witnessing domestic violence, have consistent and predictable consequences that affect many areas of functioning. These experiences engender intense affects, such as rage, betrayal, fear, resignation, defeat, and shame, and efforts to ward off the recurrence of those emotions, including the avoidance of experiences that precipitate them or engaging in behaviours that convey a subjective sense of control in the face of potential threats. These children tend to re-enact their traumas behaviourally, either as perpetrators (e.g., aggressive or sexual acting out against other children) or in frozen avoidance reactions. Their physiological dysregulation may lead to multiple somatic problems, such as headaches and stomach-aches, in response to fearful and helpless emotions.

Persistent sensitivity to reminders interferes with the development of emotional regulation and causes long-term emotional dysregulation and precipitous behaviour changes. Their over- and under-reactivity is manifested on multiple levels: emotional, physical, behavioural, cognitive, and relational. They have fearful, enraged, or avoidant emotional reactions to minor stimuli that would have no significant effect on secure children. After having become aroused, these children have a great deal of difficulty restoring homeostasis and returning to baseline. Insight and understanding about the origins of their reactions seems to have little effect.

In addition to the conditioned physiological and emotional responses to reminders characteristic of PTSD, children with complex trauma develop a view of the world that incorporates their betrayal and hurt. They anticipate and expect the trauma to recur and respond with hyperactivity, aggression, defeat, or freeze responses to minor stresses. Cognition in these children is also affected by reminders of the trauma. They tend to become confused, dissociated, and disorientated when faced with stressful stimuli. They easily misinterpret events in the direction of a return of trauma and helplessness, which causes them to be constantly on guard, frightened, and over-reactive.

In addition, expectations of a return of the trauma permeate their relationships. This is expressed as negative self-attributions, loss of trust in caretakers, and loss of the belief that some somebody will look after them and make them feel safe. They tend to lose the expectation that they will be protected and act accordingly. As a result, they organize their relationships around the expectation or prevention of abandonment or victimization. This is expressed as excessive clinging, compliance, oppositional defiance, and distrustful behaviour. They also may be preoccupied with retribution and revenge.

All of these problems are expressed in dysfunction in multiple areas of functioning: educational, familial, peer-related, legal, and work-related.

Treatment implications

In the treatment of traumatized children and adolescents, there often is a painful dilemma of whether to keep them in the care of people or institutions who are sources of hurt and threat, or whether to play into abandonment and separation distress by taking the child away from familiar environments and people to whom they are intensely attached but who are likely to cause further substantial damage (Streeck-Fischer & van der Kolk, 2000). Treatment must focus on three primary areas: establishing safety and competence, dealing with traumatic re-enactments, and integration and mastery of the body and mind.

Establishing safety and competence

Complexly traumatized children need to be helped to engage their attention in pursuits that do not remind them of trauma-related triggers and that give them a sense of pleasure and mastery. Safety, predictability, and "fun" are essential for the establishment of the capacity to observe what is going on, put it into a larger context, and initiate physiological and motoric self-regulation.

Before addressing anything else, these children need to be helped how to react differently from their habitual fight/flight/freeze reactions (Streeck-Fischer & van der Kolk., 2000). Only after children develop the capacity to focus on pleasurable activities without becoming disorganized do they have a chance to develop the capacity to play with other children, engage in simple group activities, and deal with more complex issues.

Dealing with traumatic re-enactments

After a child is traumatized multiple times, the imprint of the trauma becomes lodged in many aspects of his or her makeup. This is manifested in multiple ways: fearful reactions, aggressive and sexual acting out, avoidance, and uncontrolled emotional reactions. Unless this tendency to repeat the trauma is recognized, the response of the environment is likely to replay the original traumatizing, abusive, but familiar, relationships. Because these children are prone to experience anything novel, including rules and other protective interventions, as punishments, they tend to regard teachers and therapists who try to establish safety as perpetrators (Streeck-Fischer & van der Kolk, 2000).

Integration and mastery

Mastery is most of all a physical experience: the feeling of being in charge, calm, and able to engage in focused efforts to accomplished goals. Children who have been traumatized experience the trauma-related hyper arousal and numbing on a deeply somatic level. Their hyper arousal is apparent in their inability to relax and in their high degree of irritability.

Children with "frozen" reactions need to be helped to re-awaken their curiosity and to explore their surroundings. They avoid engagement in activities because any task may unexpectedly turn into a traumatic trigger. Neutral, "fun" tasks and physical games can provide them with knowledge of what it feels like to be relaxed and to feel a sense of physical mastery.

Summary

At the centre of the therapeutic work with terrified children is helping them realize that they are repeating their early experiences and helping them find new ways of coping by developing new connections between their experiences, emotions, and physical reactions. Unfortunately, all too often, medications take the place of helping children acquire the skills necessary to deal with and master their uncomfortable physical sensations. To "process" their traumatic experiences, these children first need to develop a safe space where they can "look at" their traumas without repeating them and making them real once again (Streeck-Fischer & van der Kolk., 2000).

Note

1. This chapter is reproduced with the kind permission of the author and the publisher (Slack) of *Psychiatric Annals*.

References

Ackerman, P. T., Newton, J. E., McPherson, W. B., Jones, J. G., & Dykman, R. A. (1998). Prevalence of post traumatic stress disorder and other psychiatric diagnoses in three groups of abused children (sexual, physical, and both). *Child Abuse and Neglect*, 22(8):759–774.

American Psychiatric Association (1994). *Diagnostic and Statistical Manual of Mental Disorders* (4th edn). Washington, DC: American Psychiatric Association.

Basile, K. C., Arias, I., Desai, S., & Thompson, M. P. (2004). The differential association of intimate partner physical, sexual, psychological, and stalking violence and posttraumatic stress symptoms in a nationally representative sample of women. *Journal of Traumatic Stress*, 17(5): 413–421.

Bowlby, J. (1980). *Attachment and Loss. Vol. 3.* New York: Basic Books.

Browne, A., & Finkelhor, D. (1986). Impact of child sexual abuse: a review of the research. *Psychological Bulletin, 99*(1): 66–77.

Cicchetti, D., & Toth, S. L. (1995). Developmental psychopathology and disorders of affect. In: D. Cicchetti & D. J. Cohen (Eds.), *Developmental Psychopathology, Vol. 2: Risk, Disorder, and Adaptation* (pp. 369–420). New York: Wiley.

Cicchetti, D., & White, J. (1990). Emotion and developmental psychopathology. In: N. Stein, B. Leventhal, & T. Trebasso (Eds.), *Psychological and Biological Approaches to Emotion* (pp. 359–382). Hillsdale, NJ: Lawrence Erlbaum.

Cole, P. M., & Putnam, F. W. (1992). Effect of incest on self and social functioning: a developmental psychopathology perspective. *Journal of Consulting Clinical Psychology, 60*(2): 174–184.

Cook, A., Spinazzola, J., Ford, J. D., Lanktree, C., Blaustein, M., Cloitre, M., DeRosa, R., Hubbard, R., Kagan, R., Liataud, J., Mallah, K., Olafson, E., & van der Kolk, B. (2005). Complex trauma in children and adolescents. *Psychiatric Annals, 35*: 390–398.

Crittenden, P. M. (1992). Treatment of anxious attachment in infancy and early childhood. *Developmental and Psychopathology, 4*: 575–602.

Culp, R. E., Heide, J., & Richardson, M. T. (1987). Maltreated children's developmental scores: treatment versus non treatment. *Child Abuse and Neglect, 11*(1): 29–34.

Drossman, D. A., Leserman, J., Nachman, G., Li, Z., Gluck, H., Toomey, T. C., & Mitchell, C. M. (1990). Sexual and physical abuse in women with functional or organic gastrointestinal disorders. *Annals of Internal Medicine, 113*(11): 828–833.

Felitti, V. J., Anda, R. F., Nordenberg, D., Williamson, D. F., Spitz, A. M., Edwards, V., Koss, M. P., & Marks, J. S. (1998). The Adverse Childhood Experiences (ACE) Study. Relationship of childhood abuse and household dysfunction to many of the leading causes of death in adults. *American Journal of Preventative Medicine, 14*(4): 245–258.

Ford, J. D. (2005). Treatment implications of altered neurobiology, affect regulation and information processing following child maltreatment. *Psychiatric Annals, 35*: 410–419.

Higgins, D. J., & McCabe, M. P. (2000). Relationships between different types of maltreatment during childhood and adjustment in adulthood. *Child Maltreatment, 5*(3): 261–272.

Kegan, R. (1982). *The Evolving Self.* Cambridge, MA: Harvard University Press.

Kiser, L. J., Heston, J., Millsap, P. A., & Pruitt, D. C. (1987). Physical and sexual abuse in childhood: relationship with post-traumatic stress disorder. *American Academy of Child and Adolescent Psychiatry*, 30(5): 776–783.

Lewis, D. O., & Shanok, S. S. (1979). Perinatal difficulties, head and face trauma, and child abuse in the medical histories of seriously delinquent children. *American Journal of Psychiatry*, 136(4A): 419–423.

Piaget, J. (1954). *The Construction of Reality in the Child*. New York: Basic Books.

Pynoos, R. S., Frederick, C .J., Nader, K., Arroyo, W., Steinberg, A., Eth, S., Nunez, F., & Fairbanks, L. (1987). Life threat and post-traumatic stress in school-age children. *Archives of General Psychiatry*, 44(12): 1057–1063.

Romano, E., & De Luca, R. V. (1997). Exploring the relationship between childhood sexual abuse and adult sexual perpetration. *Journal of Family Violence*, 12(1): 85–98.

Schneider-Rosen, K., & Cicchetti, D. (1984). The relationship between affect and cognition in maltreated infants: quality of attachment and the development of visual self-recognition. *Child Development*, 55(2): 648–658.

Schore, A. (1994). *Affect Regulation and the Origin of the Self: The Neurobiology of Emotional Development*. Hillsdale, NJ: Lawrence Erlbaum.

Spinazzola, J., Ford, J. D., Zucker, M., van der Kolk, B., Silva, S., Smith, S., & Blaustein, M. (2005). Survey evaluates complex trauma exposure, outcome, and intervention among children and adolescents. *Psychiatric Annals*, 35: 433–439.

Steiner, H., Garcia, I. G., & Matthews, Z. (1997). Posttraumatic stress disorder in incarcerated juvenile delinquents. *Journal of American Academy of Child and Adolescent Psychiatry*, 36(3): 357–365.

Streeck-Fischer, A., & van der Kolk, B. (2000). Down will come baby, cradle and all: therapeutic implications of chronic trauma on child development. *Australia and New Zealand Journal of Psychiatry*, 34(6): 903–918.

Summit, R. C. (1983). The child sexual abuse accommodation syndrome. *Child Abuse and Neglect*, 7(2): 177–193.

Teicher, M. H., Andersen, S. L., Polcari, A., Anderson, C., Navalta, C., & Kim, D. (2003). The neurobiological consequences of early stress and childhood maltreatment. *Neuroscience and Biobehavioural Reviews*, 27: 33–44.

Teplin, L. A., Abram, K. M., McClelland, G. M., Dulcan, M. K., & Mericle, A. A. (2002). Psychiatric disorders in youth in juvenile detention. *Archives of General Psychiatry, 59*(12): 1133–1143.

Tucker, D. M. (1992). Developing emotions and cortical networks. In: M. R. Gunnar & C. A. Nelson (Eds.), *Minnesota Symposium on Child Psychology,* Vol. 24 (pp. 75–128). Hillsdale, NJ: Lawrence Erlbaum.

US Department of Health and Human Services, Administration on Children, Youth and Families (2003). Child Maltreatment 2001. Available at: http://www.acf.dhhs.gov/programs/cb/publications/cm01/outcover.htm.

van der Kolk, B. A. (2003). The neurobiology of childhood trauma and abuse. *Child and Adolescent Psychiatric Clinics of North America, 12*(2): 293–317.

van der Kolk, B. A. (2005). Developmental trauma disorder: towards a rational diagnosis for children with complex trauma histories. *Psychiatric Annals, 25*(5): 401–408.

van der Kolk, B.A., & Fisler, R. (1995). Dissociation and the fragmentary nature of traumatic memories: overview and exploratory study. *Journal of Traumatic Stress, 8*(4): 505–525.

van der Kolk, B. A., Roth, S., Pelcovitz, D., Mandel, F. S., & Spinazzola, J. (2008). Disorders of extreme stress: the empirical foundation of a complex adaptation to trauma. *Journal of Traumatic Stress* (in press).

Widom, C. S., & Maxfield, M. G. (1996). A prospective examination of risk for violence among abused and neglected children. *Annals of the New York Academy of Sciences, 20*: 794: 224–237.

Developmental trauma in adults: a response to Bessel van der Kolk

Felicity de Zulueta

Following Bessel van der Kolk's excellent presentation on developmental trauma in children and the resulting implications in relation to their treatment, I shall look at the implications of his presentation in relation to adult patients with a history of child abuse.

It is through an understanding of attachment disorders that we can most easily make sense of findings relating to simple and complex or developmental post traumatic stress disorder (PTSD). The implications of attachment research in terms of the assessment and treatment of psychological trauma are covered in my recent paper (Zulueta, 2006a) where I underline how PTSD impacts both on the individual and on the immediate family system and can be transmitted down the generations.

After an initial review of current research in the field of attachment, I emphasize the importance of integrating techniques that enable clients to modulate their emotions as part of the therapeutic process. These approaches are essential in the treatment of clients whose lack of affect modulation results from their early traumatization or neglect, or subsequent traumatization in adult life. These techniques influence mainly the right hemisphere through the vagus nerve; i.e., yoga breathing, the energy therapies and art and dance therapy. Eye movement desensitization and reprocessing (EMDR) and sensori-motor therapy also have an important part to play in integrating the mind and body of the traumatized individual, for whom, as van der Kolk says, the "body holds the score" (Siegel, 2001).

I end with a reference to how the abused child who becomes traumatically attached to his or her frightening care-giver continues to maintain this attachment in later life through the process of dissociation. In other words, in order to maintain their attachment to their parent, infants will develop an idealized attachment to the care-giver by dissociating off all their terrifying self–other interactions. At a cognitive level, these children will therefore blame themselves for their suffering and, thereby, retain the idealized version of their care-giver as well as retaining a sense of control and hope. Since they are to blame for their misery, there is the hope that one day, if they manage to behave better, they may finally get the love and care that they need.

This powerful cognitive defence, called the "moral defence" by Fairbairn (1952, pp. 65–67), is ferociously maintained because not only does it ward off the unbearable sense of utter helplessness that humans cannot tolerate, but it also gives the individual hope of something better. Unfortunately, it also reinforces the attachment and identification with the abusing parent, with all that this implies in terms of failure to develop adult attachment relationships and a tendency to violent and self-abusive behaviour. Addressing this "traumatic attachment" and its cognitive distortions is central to the treatment of patients with a history of child abuse (Zulueta, 2006b).

One of the most important lessons to take away from the conference is, perhaps, the importance of providing therapists in this field with peer support and supervision as well as the permission to use the affect modulating techniques not only for their patients' well-being, but also for their own.

References

Fairbairn, R. (1952). *Psychoanalytic Study of the Personality*. London: Routledge & Kegan Paul.

Siegel, D. J. (2001). Toward an interpersonal neurobiology of the developing mind: attachment relationships, "mindsight", and neural integration. *Infant Mental Health Journal*, *22*: 67–94.

Zulueta, de F. (2006a). The treatment of PTSD from an attachment perspective. *Journal of Family Therapy*, *28*: 334–351.

Zulueta, de F. (2006b). Inducing traumatic attachments in adults with a history of child abuse: forensic applications. *British Journal of Forensic Practice*, *8*: 4–15. Also available at: www.pavpub.com/pavpub/journals/BJFP/thismonthssample.pdf.

The hungry self: working with attachment trauma and dissociation in survivors of childhood abuse

Sue Richardson

This paper explores some features of attachment-based work with people with dissociative conditions. It describes work with a very wounded and vulnerable part of the self within a client, "Sally". It concludes that the capacity for repair does not rest on the severity and chronicity of abuse or developmental dependency on the abusers, but rather on establishing a secure therapeutic base from which a relational bridge (Blizard, 2003) can be built and some communication established across dissociative barriers.

Sally suffered serious attachment trauma, including emotional and sexual abuse from early childhood. She has had considerable difficulty in forming supportive companionable relationships and her relational experience has been of dominance and submission (Heard & Lake, 1997). She is also in poor physical health, much of which arises from long-term anorexia.

At the beginning of therapy, the wounded, vulnerable part of Sally was in a double bind, caught between the longing for care and the fear of approaching a care-giver. Sally regarded the emotional and physical hunger of this part of the self as dangerous and intolerable. In turn, the hungry self had become a separate, dissociated self, of whose needs and responses Sally was persistently dismissive.

The hungry self was equally avoidant of Sally and, in turn, segregated itself in response to being dismissed. Both internal and external family dynamics meant that it suffered from "Knowing what you are not supposed to know and feeling what you are not supposed to feel" (Bowlby, 1988). Nevertheless, I think this part of the self represents the healthy baby with the capacity for attachment, but who got buried and hidden because of the fear of approaching a care-giver.

The therapeutic dialogue highlighted some real difficulties: the extent of the developmental damage Sally had suffered; her intense emotional hunger for relationship and its physical counterpart; her craving for emotional proximity; her terror of this craving being misperceived (e.g., as predatory); her fear and ambivalence about responding to her physical hunger; her fear of losing her only source of identity and autonomy if she were to give up weight control; and, last, her inability to identify who might be a reliable care-giver.

The hungry self can be seen as corresponding to van der Kolk's (2005) description of developmental trauma disorder. It can be hypothesized that defensive development of neural pathways within Sally had led to the loss of connections within the right hemisphere and an inability to self-regulate. The result was a highly insecure, dissociated self who was over-reactive to stimuli and engaged in fight/flight/freeze responses. This self could not easily grasp what was going on in relationships. For example, it could not easily distinguish nurturing from non-nurturing care-givers. It longed to be taken care of but expected to be re-traumatized, and all behaviour was organized around this assumption.

I have described this kind of traumatized, dissociative self as a "little creature" who could respond to sensitive, empathic attunement and much "sitting patiently by" (Richardson, 2002). In searching for an accurate clinical term, I have wondered if it might correspond to Guntrip's (1968) "withdrawn self" or Tustin's (1972) "autistic encapsulated self". I have found that "isolated subjectivity" (Chefetz & Bromberg, 2004) most resonates with the quality of not being known or coherent. Sally had suffered a loss of innate intersubjectivity through lack of early relational exchange, but the hungry self had retained the capacity for it. My clinical experience affirms that this part of the self is not irreparably damaged and is evidence of the way in which attachment is wired in. It reminds me of the character, Natasha, in one of Gillian Slovo's novels (2004), who became emotionally frozen for an extended period of time after the traumatic loss of her partner and who, near death, is called back into life.

Initially, Sally's system as a whole corresponded to Steele, van der Hart and Nijenhuis's (2005) description of the phobia of the contents of one's own mind seen in dissociation with deficits in mentalization and affect regulation. An important effect of therapy was to re-activate Sally's attachment needs and developmental strivings. For a long time, the hungry self did not dare reflect on its own state of mind in respect of its attachment longings. Sally described this part of herself as "almost phobic of relationships". The hungry self could not believe it could be held in mind willingly by anyone, and only knew how to communicate its presence via symptoms and other problems. It took a long time in therapy (around ten years) for the hungry self to dare to emerge even partially. Essentially, time was needed to accomplish the following therapeutic tasks: to bring new experience to bear; to experience the therapeutic relationship as dependable; for Sally to be believe she had the right to a relational connection; to construct an inner working model of dyadic regulation and repair; and to attain a degree of felt security. In summary, the prior therapy involved creating a context for more secure external and internal relating in which the dissociative defences could be breached safely

Overcoming Sally's phobia of relationships led to what she termed a "crisis of attachment". She felt that first I had reached out to her and taken her by the hand Next, I had encouraged her to think about using the therapeutic relationship to form an inner supportive connection in which she could move from being persistently unresponsive to her own affective states to more attuned inner care-giving and less fearful care-seeking.

I encouraged her towards the latter prematurely. I underestimated Sally's need for prolonged affective engagement, the importance of the relational exchange in the therapy and the significance of what Steele, van der Hart, and Nijenhuis (2001) call "developmental dependency" as a route to interdependency and greater security. The course of therapy was redirected by the hungry self insisting that I remember the extent of its vulnerability and lack of both an external and internal supportive environment. I was reminded that the hungry self knew only what Sally called "obscure" (i.e., indirect and ineffective) forms of care-seeking

By choosing an anorexic solution, the hungry self had ensured its psychological survival and some form of relatedness (however indirect), but at the cost of considerable physical damage to the body. The latter was explained by Sally as an "unintended consequence". The fact that the anorexia was not meant as an attack on the body made it more difficult for the hungry self to make itself understood and placed an empathic connection within Sally even further out of reach. The hungry self could not, dared not, care-seek directly. In return, Sally could not provide care for a part whose care-seeking was both demanding and "obscure" and who was easy to perceive as predatory. The internal dynamic corresponded to Davies and Frawley's (1994) transference and countertransference matrix of the unseeing neglectful parent of the abused child. Within this dynamic, it was impossible for Sally to get into goal-corrected behaviour and her symptoms seemed intractable and endless. Any other professionals who became involved ended up voting with their feet. I was isolated, not only from them, but also from Sally in my belief in the possibility of an inner reorganization towards a more responsive and attuned system.

It is a huge challenge to remain emotionally available to Sally and other survivors who, like her, need me to be the recognizing other who can empathically enter an inner frame of reference which they themselves have disavowed and to handle the accompanying paradoxes and contradictions. For example, in Sally's case, her self-starvation has been an attempt to stay alive. There have been painful instances of Stern's (1985) true misattunement as result of my mistaking one state of mind for another or underestimating the extent of Sally's vulnerability. The empathic strain of working with Sally has been considerable. At times, I have felt like joining the professionals who voted with their feet. I think that an impulse to take flight is triggered not only by picking up on the silent suffering of parts like the hungry self, but also by having to work with opposing relational configurations within the client's system. In my experience, it can be hard to maintain a therapeutic alliance with internalized states of mind based on the original abuser, which result in the person being misattuned to their own affective states and to witness re-enactments, within the client's internal system, of unempathic, ineffective, dismissive, neglectful, or frankly abusive care-giving. In Sally's case there is a direct connection with a family history of eating disorder, but it has been her dismissal and disavowal of her hungry self as much as her self-starvation that I have found the most painful.

Good clinical supervision helps me to maintain my capacity for empathy, reflection, and self-regulation. In addition, since clients like Sally tend to have low vitality, I like to use activities directed at maintaining my own vitality levels. I have long used the kind of restorative activities advocated by Bessel van der Kolk (2004) such as yoga, tai chi, chi gung, meditation, and walking. I also feel sustained by the positive and joyful dimension of attuning to another human being, contributing to the healing process and being alongside what Sally describes as the "indomitable nature" of parts like the hungry self. This kind of affective engagement with the client at the deepest level has been described by Benatar (2004) as transformative for both client and therapist.

To return to Sally's process, following a period of countertransferential hunger, in which I ate biscuits after each session and felt anguished at watching her become increasingly frail and ill, one day I said to her, very quietly, that it would be nice to think that she could have the experience of not feeling hungry, if only once in her life. My unspoken thought was—if only once before she died—but my remark attuned to a longing for nurture and the desire to live. It was as if the hungry self pricked up its ears and decided to emerge into fuller view.

This emergence was both moving and fraught. Sally still tended to act as a dismissive care-giver, and I felt concerned about being the sole care-giver to a very isolated and vulnerable part of her, especially given the unsupportive nature of her other relationships. There were therapeutic struggles and misunderstandings. For example, Sally seemed to be saying that her hungry self had no further developmental capacity, something I found hard to accept.

Sally has always felt unable to take on inner care-giving unaided, but she can function more effectively as part of a three-way care-seeking–care-giving system via the therapy. An outcome of establishing this relational triad has been a move towards a less dismissive state, more empathic of mind towards the hungry self.

This self got the message home to me that it had to be accepted "as is", i.e., vulnerable and developmentally immature. Once this part felt affirmed in therapy, a new relationship within Sally became possible. She recognized that it was her whole self and the whole of her body that had suffered, not a separate self with a life of its own. This recognition shows the undoing of defensive exclusion (Bowlby, 1980). It has provided a basis for internal restructuring and for a shareable interpersonal world that included the hungry self as part of the whole rather than one that governed by the myth of separateness. The therapeutic dialogue has increasingly reflected Sally's changed state of mind about attachment and a shift from unformulated to formulated experience.

Since this development, the therapeutic process has been no more easy or straightforward. Sally has likened the release of her emotional and physical hunger to sitting on top of a volcano. I have found it easy to overestimate her progress, but for one thing: despite improvements in her emotional well-being and some improvement in the quality of her diet, her hungry, anorexic self has remained in evidence. "Why?" I asked myself and Sally repeatedly, "what are we missing here?"

Sally's relationship difficulties in the outside world have been a key factor in maintaining her anorexia as coping strategy. She has needed reassurance that the therapeutic relationship can remain secure with the hungry self on board and that therapy, rather than this self, can be a sufficient buffer in respect of relational problems. Sally is convinced that having the therapeutic relationship as a bridge to an inner relationship can "allay the need for the anorexia", but this needs a lot of reinforcement. Sally wants to live. She does not want to accept a slow physical decline. At the same time, meeting her emotional and physical needs for nurture simultaneously is unfamiliar and scary territory and she has referred to "closing the gap" between the two as a "tall order".

As a self who is becoming more whole, Sally has engaged in some cautious sorties into the outside world. She says that, via the therapy, she now has an alternative model of relationships to go on. She has formed a friendship based on equality rather than dominance and submission. She is becoming more assertive and less submissive at home as well as in therapy. Eating is becoming more feasible because the hungry self has some hope that there are ways other than anorexia of its presence being recognized and that support is available with the emotional dysregulation that eating brings. Sally is coping (just) with the disruption these changes are bringing to her existing relationships. She considers that the keys to her survival lie in not losing sight of her relationship with her hungry self; accepting that the altered emotional state that accompanies eating is as much part of her as any other state; that physical nurture can only follow relational nurture and ensuring that therapy continues to provide a safe haven.

My theoretical formulation of Sally's journey so far is that it reflects improved and better regulated emotional vitality and a developing sense of self attained via a long term interpersonal connection in which I hypothesize that some new neuronal connections may have been formed. Sally emphasizes the significance of the length of time we have worked together. She says it is very important to have had a long experience of continuity and consistency in therapy as a route to a more coherent internal relationship. She has moved from isolated subjectivity to intersubjectivity. Her life narrative is more coherent and less fragmented. She can communicate more directly rather than via symptoms. She has replaced her disavowal of her attachment needs with a developing theory of mind about the value of relationships. Her care-seeking and self-nurture is more effective, and she is developing a more autonomous sense of self. In her words, in the past her hungry self had "submitted to the point of non-existence and came alive in therapy".

Sally remains physically frail. She is focusing her resources on maintaining, strengthening, and consolidating the relationship with her hungry self via the therapy. To date, this triadic relationship has proved to be a sufficiently benign and responsive care-seeking–care-giving system to keep her alive. Whatever the outcome in the longer term, Sally says she is glad to have got to where she has and salutes her survival along with the therapeutic endeavour.

References

Benatar, M. (2004). Editorial: Purification and the self-system of the therapist. *Journal of Trauma and Dissociation*, 5(4): 1–15.

Blizard, R. A. (2003). Disorganised attachment, development of dissociated self-states and a relational approach to treatment. *Journal of Trauma and Dissociation*, 4(3): 27–50.

Bowlby, J. (1980). *Attachment and Loss. Vol. 3, Loss: Sadness and Depression*. London: Penguin.

Bowlby, J. (1988). On knowing what you are not supposed to know and feeling what you are not supposed to feel. In: J. Bowlby, *A Secure Base*. London: Routledge.

Chefetz, R. A., & Bromberg, P. M. (2004). Talking with 'Me' and 'Not Me': a dialogue. *Contemporary Psychoanalysis*, 40(3): 409–464.

Davies, J. M., & Frawley, M. G. (1994). *Treating the Survivor of Child Sexual Abuse: A Psychoanalytic Perspective*. New York: Basic Books.

Guntrip, H. (1968). *Schizoid Phenomena, Object Relations and the Self*. London: Hogarth.

Heard, D., & Lake, H. (1997). *The Challenge of Attachment for Caregiving*. London: Brunner-Routledge.

Richardson, S. (2002). Will you sit by her side? An attachment-based approach to work with the dissociative conditions. In: V. Sinason (Ed.), *Attachment, Trauma and Multiplicity: Working with Dissociative Identity Disorder*. London: Brunner-Routledge.

Slovo, G. (2004). *Ice Road*. New York: Little, Brown.

Steele, K., van der Hart, O., & Nijenhuis, E. R. S. (2001). Dependency in the treatment of complex posttraumatic stress disorder and dissociative disorders. *Journal of Trauma and Dissociation*, 2(4): 79–116.

Steele, K., van der Hart, O., & Nijenhuis, E. R. S. (2005). Phase-orientated treatment of structural dissociation in complex traumatization: overcoming trauma-related phobias. *Journal of Trauma and Dissociation*, 6(3): 11–53.

Stern, D. (1985). *The Interpersonal World of the Infant*. New York: Basic Books

Tustin, F. (1972). *Autism and Childhood Psychosis*. London: Hogarth.

van der Kolk, B.A (2004). The future of trauma work. *Counselling and Psychotherapy Journal*, 15 (4), 10- 13.

van der Kolk, B.A. (2005). Developmental trauma disorder: towards a rational diagnosis for children with complex trauma histories. *Psychiatric Annals*, 25(5): 401–408.

The shadow of murder: love and hate in times of violence

Rachel Wingfield

I am going to start with a clip from *Fahrenheit 9/11*, a documentary film, which includes coverage of the war in Iraq (Moore, 2004).

It will, I hope, give you just a little bit of a sense of the atmosphere, the psychic reality, inhabited by refugees from war and political violence; the processes by which ordinary people might become killers, as well as raising the question of how we adapt to living in a climate where this kind of violence and murder is commonplace.

The writer, Bertolt Brecht, captured his own experiences of living and surviving in this climate; he tells us:

> I ate my food between massacres
> The shadow of murder lay upon my sleep.
> And when I loved, I loved with indifference. (Brecht, 1947)

One of the important aspects of this conference is the explicit links we are making between different forms of trauma across the range of relational contexts, including war, cultural dislocation, both political and so-called interpersonal violence. Making these links remains a radical development, pioneered only in very recent years in Judith Herman's ground-breaking book, *Trauma and Recovery* (Herman, 1992). In this book Herman highlights that there is a need to:

> restore connections: between the public and private worlds, between the individual and community, between men and women. Trauma is about commonalities: between rape survivors and combat veterans, between battered women and political prisoners, between the survivors of vast concentration camps created by tyrants who rule nations and the survivors of small, hidden concentration camps created by tyrants who rule their homes. [p. 2–3]

So I do not want to make an arbitrary distinction between my theme today—the impact of trauma in the political sphere, abuse at the hands of the state or an authority—and Sue's theme of child abuse in the family. And, when I first began working with a survivor of political violence, what struck me were not so much the distinctions as the similarities and the resonance in the work. Both the survivors I will be talking about today were members of rebel groups fighting authoritarian regimes, both committed acts of violence as well as surviving acts of violence against them; both are also women, and experienced trauma in their family as well as at the hands of the State.

The first of these women is Nahlia, from whom I learned a great deal about surviving political violence. Nahlia was a twenty-seven-year-old Indonesian woman, who had been forced to flee Papua New Guinea two years earlier. She had been an activist in the people's solidarity movement. As one of their more prominent and daring spokespeople, Nahlia had had to leave the country after two of her close colleagues and friends in the party had been murdered by the government, and others had been imprisoned and tortured.

Nahlia was referred to me by an experienced colleague, who felt unable to work with her. "To be honest," she said to me, "I felt pretty intimidated by her."

I was intrigued. This colleague of mine was a pretty tough woman. On meeting Nahlia I was immediately aware of her strong presence in the room. She was not a big woman, only a little taller than myself, but I experienced her as physically powerful. This produced a curious body countertransference I had only come across once before, when I had briefly done some training with the army on domestic violence, and I had met an SAS officer who had recently returned from undercover work in the North of Ireland. The countertransference, if I could find a mental representation of it at all, was of being not with a human being, but with an object, a machine or a robot. I was reminded of Susie Orbach's (2002) work on the false body. This was as close as I could get to the feeling of being with her.

Early in the therapy Nahlia told me about a recurring dream she had since being forced to leave her comrades and flee Indonesia, in which she was standing naked in a walk-in wardrobe. On the coat hangers hung rows of different skins. She chose one and went outside. However, it was snowing, and even though she wore her extra skin she was naked with no clothes to protect her. Nahlia realized that this was how she had always seen herself: as going out into the world wearing extra skins to protect and conceal herself. What had led her to come into therapy was the realization that this still left her naked and out in the cold.

Nahlia's story had many layers. She grew up in a relatively wealthy family in Papua New Guinea. Her father was a prominent Marxist academic, respected by Nahlia's comrades fighting fascism. However, he had ruled the women in his family—Nahlia, her mother, and sisters—with a threatening and cruel ruthlessness. During the therapy Nahlia struggled with identifications, both with aggressor and then victim. She saw herself as the protector of her sisters and mother. At the same time she fought hard against any feeling of commonality with their vulnerability and powerlessness in the face of her father's control. She had come to identify with her father's sense of superiority in relation to politics and education and also his strength.

Further into the work, Nahlia brought a dream that had distressed her greatly. She dreamt that she was standing at a podium in a huge hall, above a crowd of thousands of people. The crowd was made up of members of every oppressed or disadvantaged group—poor, sick, raped, and discriminated against. They were all looking to Nahlia to save them. Into the room walked a figure known well to her dreams, which she named "the white devil", a huge, scaly creature, with the skin of a lizard, which was neither wholly human nor wholly a monster. It came in, terrifying the people in the room, who were screaming and sobbing on seeing it.

Nahlia felt love for the creature, and it didn't hurt her, but she knew she had to kill it in order to protect everyone else. She walked up to it, stroked its head, crying, and stuck her knife into it, killing it.

Nahlia's associations to the dream first focused on her fear of her own rage, her sense that her anger came from an identification with the aggressor who lived inside her: her father and the fascist State authorities. This enabled us to explore together what it had meant to Nahlia to become a killer herself in the context of fighting her opponents. However, as she unravelled the dream further, it became clear that she associated the white devil with a part of herself she saw as monstrous in other ways, too: full of fear, pain, and grief. Through free association, she was able to trace this creature back to her decision, at the age of six, to become a parent and protector for her mother and sisters. Before that she felt she had been a very needy child, often sick. She had then become the strong one; an identity she felt had been lost in fleeing Indonesia.

Nahlia really struggled with what she came to recognize as her own vulnerability in this dream. She found that being an aggressor was an easier thought. She began to get in touch with having had to kill off her needs to be the saviour of others. Her understanding of this dream proved to be a turning point in the work. One day she brought in her diary to read to me, in which she told me about how, as a child, she had played with butterflies, and how her father had come along and torn them up slowly in front of her. She wrote "my little soul went away so that she could play with butterflies and not have to watch them being destroyed". In the nightmare months of losing her comrades and experiencing her beloved organization being torn apart, Nahlia had re-experienced this trauma. She felt her soul had returned with the hope that through fighting for ideals they could create a world in which destruction and death were not always close at hand, only to have this hope destroyed even more painfully and finally.

This is the relational matrix that all members of a society living in the shadow of murder inhabit. Survive or be annihilated. Be a victim or an aggressor. And because we are outside of the dyad, another layer is added to this dynamic: bonds of affiliation, attachment to the wider social community. This involves added challenges. Not just how *not* to be annihilated, but how to respond to the imminent threat to others. Are you going to be a bystander, witness, collaborator, or saviour? The shadow of a murderous environment is that to fight it means having to engage with that reality head-on every day. This throws up the dilemma of how to do that without distancing or objectifying the people harmed as victims; how to hold on to that potential victim status without falling apart.

In all the survivors of political violence and torture I have worked with, there lives a pervasive sense of guilt, a feeling of having been contaminated by the perpetrator's brutality and violence, what Sue Grand calls in *The Reproduction of Evil* (2002), "malignant contagion". She writes that:

> In conditions of terror and oppression, the fullness of the victim's ethical integrity is rarely sustained unless she quickly succumbs to death. When death is not swift, the victim must live in negotiation with the imminence of annihilation: courage and ruthlessness become inseparable. [p. 112]

The sense of having betrayed oneself to survive is, in my experience, always linked to having betrayed the other—it is part of a relational context. This arose particularly intensely in my work with Leah, a client who was a torture survivor. We had been working together for six years when we both felt the therapy was nearing its end. However, the stumbling block for Leah remained the feeling that, in her most desperate moment, she had proved her torturers were right. Under the influence of severe torture and threat of death, she was forced to renounce her ideals, and then to laugh and joke about someone else as they were being tortured. She told me that for a moment she meant it: unable to hold on to her beliefs, relieved to be joining in with her abusers, having contempt for others being tortured.

I felt so much compassion towards her when she told me this. But at times I was drawn into the despair induced by her captors, wondering if anything that happened between us could help Leah let go of her survivor guilt here.

I got frustrated with what at times seemed like her insistence on clinging to a perception of herself as a perpetrator, a stubborn refusal to let it go and understand her response as a normal human response to the limitations in which she found herself.

Eventually, I found myself becoming angry in the room with her, as a cold, aggressive voice told me yet again that I simply did not understand that they had won, she had become like them, she was just as bad as they were, she had to live with that.

I told her that for some reason she wanted to convince herself of that, it got her into some kind of comfort zone of punishing herself. I did not believe that her torturers had taken her soul, but she was certainly choosing to identify with them now.

For the first time Leah became openly enraged with me. How dare I suggest she WANTED to be like her torturers? How dare I suggest she had any choice in this now? She had given in and they had brain-washed her: it was too late.

That statement, that it was "too late", brought us both up short. We sat in silence until I said gently, "Leah, I think part of you needs to believe it's too late. Can't bear the thought that you might start living again, because you feel you don't deserve it. You think you should have died like some of the other prisoners. To make up for the fact that there are other people out there being tortured, and you can't do anything to stop it. At least while you think you are like the torturers you can have some impact, and you can have a reason to punish and hate yourself."

She began to cry.

And after this session, Leah brought me a story she had written called "The Guardian of the Book". It was a story of a young woman, who lived in a dangerous land, in which the good rulers were about to be swept away by evil colonialists. Just as the soldiers of the new regime were about to take power, Leah was handed a book by the leader.

"This book contains the secrets of our land, our customs, our own ways of being; we will need it when we come back into power. You must guard it for us. If the book were then destroyed we would be wiped out forever."

For the next ten years Leah guarded the book safely and kept it hidden. Then one glorious day she heard that the good guys were winning their war against the oppressors and were about to come back to power. The day they reclaimed the city, she was called by the new government to bring back the book so that their land could be reinstated. On the way to their camp, Leah had to swim across a river, and nearly drowned; she dropped the book and it fell to the bottom of the water. She arrived at the camp devastated and confessed. The Leader took her aside.

"I really don't think you need to worry Leah," he said. "We know you did your best." "But I lost the book, our most important secrets, the things that made us unique." The Leader paused, "But Leah, you kept the book for ten years. Didn't you read it?" Leah stared at him. "Well yes, of course." "Do you remember what you read?" "Of course I do." "Well Leah, we don't need the book. Just tell us."

In the session Leah and I were both still. At first she had not seen what she had written. Then she realized: part of her had kept safe everything she needed to know; even when she appeared to have lost herself, somewhere inside her soul, her subjectivity was still there: no one had been able take it from her.

With Leah, I learned that on coming up against the identification with the aggressor I needed to liberate myself from Leah's sense of being colonized and her terror of confronting her torturers. I needed to allow myself to find my anger at being trapped with her torturers in that place of despair.

Torture survivors have experienced on a profound level the reality of subject–object relating, a sustained attempt to annihilate their subjectivity.

Healing this calls for a relational, responsive therapist. The so-called neutrality of the blank screen or silent therapist can be re-traumatizing in this context. Leah had had this experience with a previous therapist. The silence, the waiting, re-evoked for her, in the transference, memories of lying for hours alone in a room, waiting for one of the torturers to return. It also evoked the trauma of their silence in response to her screams and their seeming inability to react to her pleas for release, her repeated attempts to appeal to their humanity and get them to see *her* as human. What she needed from me was an authentic human encounter.

Unless attachment feelings and needs are evoked in a long-term relationship where intersubjectivity is again possible, survivors can easily retreat behind their defences against forming relationships again: this is why attachment-based therapy is particularly needed. Other options outside of the relational matrix of victim, aggressor, bystander, must be made available, in which the therapist, no matter what, forces herself out of this relational bind and frees herself from the dynamic the survivor places her in.

So, what chance has love in this context? Nahlia and Leah had lived as outsiders in their own country, outcasts, alienated from their families. That sense of being outside was intensified on so many internal and external levels with the experience of being forced to flee here as refugees. Nahlia's only secure attachment bonds had been in the party. How can we understand the intensity of bonds between survivors? "War buddies", people who have been involved in fighting together? These bonds can make the difference between coming out of the situation with PTSD or not, between breaking down or being able to grieve and move on.

Conversely, an experience, or perception, of betrayal at the hands of our allies or comrades can bring us closest to feeling that our capacity to hope and trust, our very ability to attach and connect to others, has been destroyed for ever.

I was reminded of visiting Kilmainham jail in Dublin, last year. This was the site of the executions of the leaders of the 1916 uprising, whose deaths inspired such feelings of love and loyalty in the Irish people that this seeming defeat led to an even stronger movement and, ultimately, to independence from Britain. However, it is also the site of the incarceration of Anne Devlin, who was imprisoned for her involvement in the 1803 uprising, kept in solitary confinement, and horrifically tortured for the names of the other rebels. When she refused to give their names, members of her family were captured and brought to the prison and tortured as well; seven of them died. Despite her youth and the brutality of the experience, Anne did not betray her comrades and was eventually released. Far from being greeted and thanked or rewarded by her comrades, she was ostracized by the Republican community, and died penniless and isolated on the streets. So why did this happen?

Nahlia told me similar stories, including her own rejection of any kind of vulnerability in her allies, and her avoidance of anyone who seemed to be struggling or falling apart. Most painfully, she described her cadre turning on one another, those seen as more influential or powerful being the focus for caucusing, envy, paranoia, and hate. In particular, she was haunted by a memory of having undermined one of her friends during a meeting, accusing him of being a sell-out to the cause. He was captured later that week and she never saw him again. She also recalled a long-term comrade reporting her for having, he thought, given away a party secret to an outsider. The experience had left her determined that she would never again try to fight for ideals, unsure if there was anything or anyone worth fighting for.

In our work together on this, Nahlia and I came to distinguish between survivor bonds, strong alliances formed in the context of fighting back, and victim bonds, relationships between those who feel powerless and defeated in trying to change their situation. We began to understand how the bonds in Nahlia's political network shifted back and forth between these different dynamics, according to the pressures the party was under.

As therapists, the nature of the attachments in abusive families are familiar to us. Rarely are non-abusive family members bonded together in a loving alliance, able to stand up for one another when they are the one being scapegoated. More often than not, victims are forced into having to let one another down to survive. Stay quiet while the other one is abused, otherwise it will be you next; join in with the abuser in putting down another member of the family, because it might win you some favours. These bonds can become entangled, enmeshed, with shared defences and evasions that justify the family culture. This can mirror the bonds in political movements and in refugee communities: to have searched for belonging, found and then lost it, can feel like a final nail in the coffin of hope. Survivors in political movements have to endure a terrible sense of disappointment in one another and themselves. The sense of failure can be enormous: failure to nurture each other, or save each other, failure to hate the violence more than each other when disappointments hit. The work with Nahlia made us both wonder how we can find a way to forgive our heroes and freedom movements for failing to rescue us from pain.

The extent of the emotional deprivation in these groups and cultures fighting in the shadow of murder hit me powerfully. Survival and the cause are what matters. It can be viewed as self-indulgent to take care of yourself and each other in this situation, and also impossible. Scrabbling for scant resources from one another, not able to provide for the intense deprivation and not even being sure what is missing, can lead to bitter and heart-breaking dynamics.

To keep focused on the enemy is hard. Instead, the one that raises the hope or expectation becomes the focus for all the disappointment and rage—but you said you would save me; you said there would be no more pain; you said there would be justice and equality and I still feel terrible, I still don't feel loved, why aren't you/the leaders/comrades saving me? There is an enormity of an unmourned shared history, where whole cultures and communities have endured living with that sense of betrayal and abandonment. For both Nahlia and Leah, it was a long, agonizing journey, requiring as much courage as their original survival of trauma, to get to a point of forgiving themselves and their movements for the pain, losses, and failures they had endured together and at times inflicted on one another.

I'd like to end with some words from Brecht (1947) about his own experiences in political movements:

> For we knew only too well:
> Even the hatred of squalor
> Makes the brow grow stern.
> Even anger against injustice
> Makes the voice grow harsh. Alas, we
> Who wished to lay the foundations of kindness
> Could not ourselves be kind.
> But you, when at last it comes to pass
> That man can help his fellow man,
> Do not judge us
> Too harshly.

References

Brecht, B. (1947). "To Posterity". In: *Selected Poems* (H. R. Hays, Trans.). New York: Harcourt.

Grand, S. (2002). *The Reproduction of Evil: A Clinical and Cultural Perspective*. Hillside, NJ: Analytic Press.

Herman, J. L. (1992). *Trauma and Recovery: The Aftermath of Violence — From Domestic Abuse to Political Terror*. New York: Basic Books.

Moore, M. (Dir.) (2004). *Fahrenheit 9/11*. Lion Gate Films.

Orbach, S. (2002) Revisiting the false self. In: B. Kahr (Ed.), *The Legacy of Winicott*. London: Karnac.

How do we help ourselves?

Valerie Sinason

Introduction

[As people came back from their final break of the conference, Valerie had Vusi Mahlesela's haunting "When you come back" playing in the auditorium. Written to inspire Mandela's return from prison, the piece starts in enormous sadness and moves into deep celebration. It was played both as an example of music chosen by Valerie to help herself and as a link to Gillian Slovo's moving talk on South Africa at the start of the conference.]

Here to welcome you in was music from Vusi Mahlesela which helps me and inspires me, linking me with my yearly work in Cape Town and here. Music was an important expression of emotional and political resolve, longing and pain in South Africa, and is one of the ways many of us help ourselves. Some of us, like Brett Kahr and John Southgate, take it further by being professional musicians!

I would also like to say something I promised to say to the small group I facilitated. This has been a powerful and demanding conference and if anyone has had enough and would like to help themselves by saying "no" to any more input, please do leave now! Some of us find it very hard to help ourselves to regulate work input and politely go beyond our tolerance level!

Helping ourselves, as people who work with vulnerable people.

First of all, in having this title I must apologize to all those with chronic complex traumatic experiences, because it takes a remarkable amount of generosity to cope with the concept of a title like this, to consider what resources and support a clinician needs, when the clinician is lucky enough to maintain themselves adequately enough to have a job and function in it.

The American disability movement calls non-disabled people the "temporarily unimpaired". Perhaps we need to call ourselves, as practising clinicians, the temporarily untraumatized. For who knows what tsunami of the soul, of politics, of family life, of our bodies and minds can hit us by surprise while we live in the hope of a safe trajectory. At any moment a "strange attractor" can remove us from our capacity to work.

As a child and adult therapist, I have worked with the distressed and dispossessed in prisons, residential units, hospitals, and schools for the maladjusted, here and in Scandinavia, Europe, and especially in African townships and at the Clinic for Dissociative Studies, which I founded after leaving the Tavistock Clinic in 1998. (I left when it became clear that no unit could be established there for working with ritual abuse and dissociative clients outside of research grants.)

I and colleagues are regularly told by clients, even by those who ring in a desperate helpline way, that we have been drip-fed traumatic narratives; we are watched to see if we retaliate, get ill, give up. Only when we show we are still standing is it possible for the next drip to be given. Indeed, one survivor commented that the tension in therapy was how long the client had to wait for the therapist to be able to bear to hear them. Another has commented that I am her long-term investment, and after spending so much time training me it is not worth leaving me to start the process all over again with someone else, however unsatisfactory I am. And when we reel from the tiny drip the client has tested on us, what does it feel to be that person, that client? To be the one with the tale that cannot be totally given because the words and feelings hurt and kill?

So, a paradoxical truth has to be voiced that we also look after ourselves by working with our clients, who support us and are in the same political battle as us for recognition of their trauma. I think we also help ourselves by doing the work. By being there, in whatever way we manage, we are not being the non-innocent bystander, as Petruska Clarkson so superbly put it. We are there, and then do not suffer witness guilt, in Judith Herman's (1992) terms.

What are we hearing? In the first place we are hearing narratives of torture: torture within families and neighbourhoods, in schools, in churches, mosques, graveyards, cellars, woods; experiences which are not considered true. These are the invisible refugees, the discredited refugees. Murder, cannibalism, necrophilia, bestiality, starvation, oral, anal, vaginal abuse, grievous bodily harm, infanticide. We can give a formal list of Latinate words of legal offences, but that does not convey the terror. And then we are hearing of children broken into fragments through overwhelming torture from attachment figures who become adults with multiple minds in one body.

Patients come with one voice, saying there was this childhood, nothing much to say, perhaps one caretaker was abusive but they have left all that behind. And slowly you meet the others and find the abuse is not over, it is ongoing, that you are communicating with a brave citizen who knows they are sitting on the burial ground of a massacre but does not know who the perpetrators are, and children and adolescents who do.

Safety is the first step, Herman (1992), has said. But what about when we are working with those who are not safe and cannot be safe and may never be safe. May never be "cured", may never integrate, may never be co-conscious, and may be stuck in domestic abuse torture in multiple myriad ways with a terrible twist—not knowing who hurts them or where or when psychic autonomy will go.

"I walk along the street and I am in pain in my body but I do not know who has caused it. Different men and women smile at me in the day. Do they know me? Are they abusing me? Will I see this moment through until I get home or will I disappear and find myself bruised and bleeding a few hours later."

So how do we help ourselves when we are listening to narratives like that. Well, I have several different answers. But the first is that we cannot.

I have the beginnings of a cold after several late night calls to people suffering the calendar abuse that this time of the year represents. I usually work a thirteen-hour day, try to be available for most significant dates in the year, and my mother wonders why I couldn't have stayed enjoying my previous dissociative life of leaving the office for August with little thought for the attachment systems that were mobilized by my absence and going home at normal hours each day.

You see, an irony is that the more we distance ourselves as clinicians the more well we can feel. But it is a wellness born of a false self-compliance to training ideas. The more we feel and hear the less well we initially become. If we see clients that we find comfortable, that do not knock our assumptions and framework, then we are not feeling close to trauma, we are dissociating. Really feeling close to the spirit of the other, whether victim, perpetrator, or victim–perpetrator, in the way Gillian Slovo described the intimacy involved in meeting the murderers of her mother, means our own known zone is extended. As Nietzsche comments, "Beware—when you look into the abyss—the abyss looks into you". So we have to accept a different vision of the world, a world that allows such things to happen. That enlarges our souls and capacities, but it means taking in cruelty and pain on a level we may never have experienced.

Humour is a wonderful release. In a session with a Dissociative Identity Disordered (DID) patient, the main personality warned me that an alter had been programmed to commit suicide. I completely lost this crucial piece of information and the session ended without that alter appearing. At the end of the session the patient said, "You are saying goodbye to me. You haven't seen John [not the real name] have you?" I said no. "And you knew he was programmed to commit suicide, and it is a bad night and you are letting us go." I stood there reeling, slowly aware of my omission. Then the patient burst out laughing. "I don't believe it, Valerie. You are dissociative." We both burst out laughing. She is one of the main reasons I am now aware of how some trainings, though not CAPP, bring up dissociative therapists.

Working in a less dissociative way involves a transparency that can be frightening to begin with, until we can embrace it. A woman with DID came with one sadistic alter that mocked my cowardice each week. "I read a book on a serial killer for relaxation. It was so simple." One week she came frightened; a change had happened. She had a flashback she wanted to discuss. "I went to my uncle . . . there was this boy there . . . a little cousin . . . I . . . er . . ." To my shock I felt an aggression in myself, an inner voice that was saying, "Yes, well, we know you hurt him." "What are you frightened of saying?" I said, in as calm a tone as possible. "I wonder if I can help you . . . you find it hard to speak of the little boy . . ." She knew what was under my voice. She stood up and screamed at me "Alright you bitch, you know what I did, I hurt him. Satisfied?" I apologized. I said she had picked up something aggressive perhaps under my tone of voice. I said I could see how she kept this hard persona to deal with the pain she felt, and the one time she came in a softer way I picked up that tone as a defence. She sat down again and we could carry on working. Such clients have been stripped through their skin and souls and know when we have added on any layers.

Gillian Slovo's literary work brilliantly links the personal narrative and political one through writing. Susie Orbach, in last night's discussion, raised the issue of whether writing was a way of working through. For me it certainly is.

So even though love, friendship, therapy, supervision, walks, the luxury of buying a Jacuzzi as a fiftieth birthday present, were and are important, for me writing is a major way of looking after myself. In writing I am also attached to my father, who was a writer. So I inherited a typewriter as a transitional object. When writing I experience enormous peace no matter what I am writing. I am linked to the best of myself generationally.

Writing papers and workbooks allows me to not feel isolated from colleagues whose clinical techniques have not had to be tested in the same foundry. It keeps me theoretically in touch and helps to minimize the defensive narcissism that can occur when your subject matter is discredited. But I have to say a certain arrogance remains to aid me! And I owe this to John Bowlby. When I organised his eightieth birthday party for the Association of Child Psychotherapists, I asked what was the best of being eighty, and he said,

"To see my enemies have to admit I was right!" I am determined to see that through.

And I also write poems that aid me in wholeness.

So I will read some poems that link with clinical experience.

I will start with South Africa, which also helps me look after myself. I go there for a holiday to work in the University of Cape Town's Child Guidance Unit primarily. It organizes and supports pioneering township projects, and I come back invigorated by the privilege. On my last visit in one weekend there were thirty burials of people who had died from Aids. In Soweto it was 150.

In going to a township project in Cape Town to help train some volunteers as handicap and abuse counsellors, I sat in a large group. A colleague began to introduce the project, suggesting an introductory game. "My name is Mary and to get here today I left my breakfast dishes in the sink and did not make my bed." A student followed that with "I left my teddy bear on my pillow and missed my favourite soap." Then came a volunteer. "I am Sweetness. I left six children in the Transkei with my grandmother. I hope she is alive. I left my baby in Khayelitsha with my sister. I hope no-one has hurt them." After thirty such dramatically contrasting biographies something very different was alive in the room. The student repeating a safe encounter group game of introductions never expected responses to yield such pain.

Women's voices from township seminars in Cape Town

(With love to the women of Empelweni.)

(1)

> I am Pumza
> I left five children in Mitchell Plains
> To come here to study today
> My son took money to school
> To pay the gangsters
> I hope they won't shoot him

(2)

> I am Sweetness
> I left a baby two months old
> In Transkei
> The milk leaks from my breasts
> My husband is sick
> My grandmother is old
> I hope she can look after them

(3)

> I am Charity
> I left my strong heart
> In the taxi rank at Khayelitsha
> Gun-shot sent it away from me
> And it has not returned

(4)

> I am Ruth
> I left my mother Naomi
> to die in the hospital
> We had no money for burial
> Now I drink bleach
> And try to join her

(5)

> I am Mary
> I left my pass
> Like an old skin
> At Khayelitsha
> And the street committee
> Swept it up
> And cleaned me

(6)

> I am Zaniywe
> I have a headache,
> My eyes need glasses
> I gave them to my sister today
> Her eyes were so red and sore.

Poverty
It is all relative.

At night it is cold.
My eyes hurt.
A book is expensive.
I have family to support

But I have a door.
I can close the door of my shack.
I have a candle to read from
This is Africa

(7)

I am Zibonele
I restore the children
I am Ethenembi
I remake arms and legs
I am Siyazama
I smooth hurt brains
I am Empelweni
I re-member

(8)

Washing on Kayelitsha—white, so white
So stretched and distended
So full of holes
So clean and sparkling.

Here is a poem written when working with a man with Alzheimer's disease. It was written shortly before he died.

Alzheimer's disease

He sits with his head in his hands
on the stiff armchair

In the spare bedroom
the old help sleeps

Together they have watched the house
empty itself

The children left the house
like a flock of birds

The leaves left the trees

Even the cars left the street
leaving the houses like thin stalks

And his brain is leaving him
Each day it erases itself
his sentences end in a silver trail

A daily funeral

Yesterday all place names left him forever
Today it was numbers

the shadow of an atlas crosses his face
Today the old help forgets to make
him lunch
Today he forgot he had not eaten

Touching the family photographs
like a fading braille

He sits holding his head
on the stiff armchair

Treating Satanist abuse survivors

(1)

In the garden
A green breath rises and rises
I am sitting by the window
On the table your fax
Sends murder down the lines

(2)

In the hospital
A woman asks for drugs
A child is dying through her mouth
Neither of them can rest

(3)

In the morgue
The dead child is calling for her mother
As we write
The scars on her head close
Like red zips

(4)

In the wood
Dead doghairs grow flesh
Whimper
Then howl for a kennel

(5)

We put these things together
Together we find a voice

References

Herman, J. (1992). *Trauma and Recovery: The Aftermath of Violence from Domestic Abuse to Political Terror*. New York: Basic Books.

Trauma and attachment reading list

Books

Bizos, G. (1998). *No One to Blame? In Pursuit of Justice in South Africa.* Cape Town: David Philip/Mayibuye Books.

Bloom, S. (1997). *Creating Sanctuary: Toward the Evolution of Sane Societies.* London: Routledge.

Bromberg, P. M. (2001). *Standing in the Spaces: Essays on Clinical Process, Trauma and Dissociation.* New York: Analytic Press.

Cozolino, L. (2002).*The Neuroscience of Psychotherapy: Building and Rebuilding the Human Brain.* London: Norton.

Dangor, A. (2004). *Bitter Fruit.* London: Atlantic Books.

Davies, J. M., & Frawley, M. G. (1994). *Treating the Adult Survivor of Childhood Sexual Abuse: A Psychoanalytic Perspective.* New York: Basic Books.

De Kock, E. (1998). *A Long Night's Damage: Working for the Apartheid State.* Saxonwold, South Africa: Contra Press.

De Zulueta, F. (2006). *From Pain to Violence, The Roots of Human Destructiveness.* Chichester: Wiley.

Etherington, K. (Ed.) (2003). *Trauma, the Body and Transformation: A Narrative Inquiry.* London: Jessica Kingsley.

Foa, E. B. Keane, T.M., & Friedman, M. J. (2004). *Effective Treatments for PTSD: Practice Guidelines from the International Society for Traumatic Stress Studies*. New York: Guilford.

Gobodo-Madikizela, P. (2002). *A Human Being Died That Night*. New York: Houghton Mifflin.

Heard, D., & Lake, H. (1997). *The Challenge of Attachment for Caregiving*. London: Brunner-Routledge.

Herman, J. (1992). *Trauma and Recovery: The Aftermath of Violence from Domestic Abuse to Political Terror*. New York: Basic Books.

Krog, A. (1999). *Country of My Skull. Guilt, Sorrow, and the Limits of Forgiveness in the New South Africa*. London: Jonathan Cape.

McCluskey, U. (2005). *To Be Met as a Person: The Dynamics of Attachment in Professional Encounters*. London: Karnac.

Mollon, P. (1996*). Multiple Selves, Multiple Voices: Working with Trauma, Violation and Dissociation*. Chichester: Wiley.

Ney, P. N., & Peters, A. (1995). *Ending the Cycle of Abuse, the Stories of Women Abused as Children and the Group Therapy Techniques that Helped them Heal*. New York: Brunner-Mazel.

Richardson, S., & Bacon, H. (Eds.) (2001). *Creative Responses to Child Sexual Abuse: Challenges and Dilemmas*. London: Jessica Kingsley.

Shapiro, F. (2002). *EMDR as an Integrative Psychotherapy Approach: Experts of Diverse Orientations Explore the Paradigm Prism*. Washington, DC: American Psychological Association Press.

Sinason, V. (Ed.) (2002). *Attachment, Trauma and Multiplicity: Working with Dissociative Identity Disorder*. London: Brunner-Routledge.

Slovo, G. (1997). *Every Secret Thing: My Family, My Country*. London: Abacus.

Slovo, G. (2002). *Red Dust*. London: Virago.

Solomon, J., & George, C. (1999). *Attachment Disorganization*. New York: Guilford.

Solomon, M. F., & Siegel, D. J. (2003). *Healing Trauma: Attachment, Mind, Body and Brain*. London: Norton.

Stern, D. (1985). *The Interpersonal World of the Infant*. New York: Basic Books.

van der Kolk, B. A., McFarlane, A.C., & Weisaeth, L. (1996). *Traumatic Stress: the Effects of Overwhelming Experience on Mind, Body, and Society*. New York: Guilford.

Articles

Fonagy, P., & Target, M. (1997). Attachment and reflective function: their role in self organisation. *Development and Psychopathology, 9*: 679–700.

Hesse, E., & Main, M. (2000). Disorganized infant, child and adult attachment; collapse in behavioural and attention strategies. *Journal of the American Psychoanalytic Association*, 48:1097–1127.

Perry, B. (1995). Childhood trauma, the neurobiology of adaption and "use dependent" development of the brain: how "states" become "traits". *Infant Mental Health Journal*, 16: 271–291.

Purnell, C. (2004). Attachment theory and attachment-based therapy. In: M. Green & M. Coles (Eds.), *Attachment and Human Survival*. London: Karnac.

Richardson, S., & Bacon, H. (2001). Attachment theory and child abuse: an overview of the literature for practitioners. *Child Abuse Review*, 10(6): 377–397.

Schore, A. N. (1996). Experience dependent maturation of a regulatory system in the orbital pre-frontal cortex and the origin of developmental psychopathology. *Development & Psychopathology*, 8: 59–87.

Siegel, D. J. (2001). Toward an interpersonal neurobiology of the developing mind: attachment relationships, "mindsight", and neural integration. *Infant Mental Health Journal*, 22: 67–94.

van der Kolk, B. A. (1994). The body keeps the score: Memory and the emerging psychobiology of post traumatic stress. *Harvard Review of Psychiatry*, 1: 253–265.

van der Kolk, B. A. (2002). *The Assessment and Treatment of Complex PTSD*.In R. Yehuda (Ed.) *Treating Trauma Survivors with PTSD*. Washington, DC: American Psychiatric Press.

van der Kolk, B. A. (2005). Developmental trauma disorder. *Psychiatric Annals*, 401–408.

van der Kolk, B. A., & Fisler, R. (1995). Dissociation and the fragmentary nature of traumatic memories: overview and exploratory study. *Journal of Traumatic Stress*, 8: 505–525.

van der Kolk, B. A., Pelcovitz, D., Roth, S., Mandel, F. S., McFarlane, A., & Herman, J. L. (1996). Dissociation, somatization, and affect dysregulation: the complexity of adaptation of trauma. *American Journal of Psychiatry*, 153(Suppl): 83–93.

Vas Dias, S. (2004). Cumulative phobic response to early traumatic attachment: aspects of a developmental psychotherapy in midlife. *Journal of Attachment and Human Development*, 6(2):163–179.

Zulueta, de F. (1999). Borderline personality disorder as seen from an attachment perspective: a review. *Criminal Behaviour and Mental Health*, 9: 237–253.

Zulueta, de F. (2006). The treatment of psychological trauma from the perspective of attachment research. *Journal of Family Therapy*, *28*(4): 334–351.

Zulueta, de F. (2006). Inducing traumatic attachments in adults with a history of child abuse: forensic applications. *British Journal of Forensic Practice*, *8*: 4–15

Other resources

Website of the Boston Trauma Centre can be found at www.trauma-center.org. Articles of Professor B. van der Kolk and colleagues can be downloaded from this very informative site.

Journal of Traumatic Stress (2005). *18*(5): A special issue on complex trauma.

Introduction to The Centre for Attachment-based Psychoanalytic Psychotherapy

The Centre for Attachment-based Psychoanalytic Psychotherapy (CAPP) is an organization committed to the development of this particular approach to psychotherapy. It provides a four-year training for psychotherapists and a consultation and referral service.

Attachment-based psychoanalytic psychotherapy has developed on the basis of the growing understanding of the importance of attachment relationship to human growth and development throughout life. This approach to psychotherapy, developing from the relational tradition of psychoanalysis, draws upon psychoanalytic insights and the rapidly growing field of attachment theory.

Understanding psychotherapy within the context of attachment relationships leads to an approach to psychotherapy as a co-operative venture between therapist and client. The aim is to develop a sufficiently secure base to enable the exploration of loss and trauma in the course of development. The therapy is designed to create a safe space in which the client can reflect upon their lived experience, their experience of relationships in the present, and their experience of their relationship with the therapist.

Mourning is vital to the acknowledgement and understanding of the effects of abandonment, loss, abuse, whether emotional, sexual, or physical. The support of an authentic process of mourning forms a central part of the therapeutic work. This is crucial to the development of a sense of self, and the capacity to form and sustain intimate relationships. Both a strong sense of self and good attachment relationships are essential to managing stressful experiences.

The losses and traumas to be addressed in therapy are not confined to a private world or to early life. Groups and society as a whole shape attachment relationships formed by individuals. The experience of loss and abuse as a result of structures and pressures and everyday experiences concerning race, gender, sexuality, class, culture, and disability, together with the complexity of the individual's response, can be worked with in a profound way through attachment-based psychoanalytic psychotherapy.

John Bowlby's original development of attachment theory was promoted primarily by his concern to ensure social recognition for the central importance of attachment and the experience of loss in early development. He was also concerned to strengthen the scientific foundations for psychoanalysis. Since his original work attachment theory has come to occupy a key position in this fast growing scientific field. Attachment theory provides a crucial link between psychoanalysis, developmental psychology, neurobiology, and the behavioural sciences.

CAPP has drawn on a wide range of approaches including the British Object Relations tradition, American Relational Psychoanalysis, theories on the development of the self, and contemporary work on trauma and dissociation to provide a breadth and depth of insight into the structure and dynamics of the internal world. The common themes that run through them all are the importance of unconscious communication, of the transference and the countertransference, of containment and the acceptance of difference, and an emphasis on two-person psychology.

The development of our theoretical base is a dynamic and continuing process. The Centre will continue to adapt and develop in the light of new research, contemporary developments and clinical experience.

We run a clinical training course, short courses and edit a professional journal called *ATTACHMENT: New Perspectives on Psychotherapy and Relational Psychoanalysis*, published by Karnac.

Trustees of CAPP

Mohamud Ahmed
Elaine Arnold
Sir Richard Bowlby (Chair of Trustees)
James Sainsbury

Chair of CAPP

Rachel Wingfield

Vice Chair

Emerald Davies

Address

Centre for Attachment-based Psychoanalytic Psychotherapy
The John Bowlby Centre
147 Commercial Street
London E1 6BJ

Tel: 020 247 9101

Email address:
administrator@attachment.org.uk

Website:
www.johnbowlbycentre.org.uk

CAPP is a Registered Charity, No. 1064780/0
and a Company Limited by Guarantee, No. 3272512

9781855756663